Turning Inspiration into Action

How to connect to the powers you need to conquer negativity, act on the best opportunities, and live the life of your dreams

by Matt Gersper

FOREWORD BY KEITH NORRIS

Happy Living

Published in the United States by
Happy Living Books Independent Publishers
www.happyliving.com/books

Copyright 2016 by Matthew Brian Gersper

Researched and written by Matthew Brian Gersper
Edited by Kelly McKain
Cover art by Suzana Stankovic

For permission requests, please contact:
matt@happyliving.com

Printed in the United States of America
ISBN: 978-0-9994771-4-4

Other Books by Happy Living

www.happyliving.com/books

Finding Your Black Belt (2018)
by Karen Conover

Inspiring Women (2017)
by Matt Gersper

The Greener The Grass (2017)
by Scott Barry

Love Letters from the Grave (2016)
by Dr. Paul Gersper

The Belief Road Map (2016)
by Matt Gersper and Kaileen Elise Sues

Join Our Community

Join our community to stay informed of upcoming books, promotions, and weekly inspiration from Happy Living!

We are on a mission to improve the health and wellbeing of the world, one person at a time.

Our blog is packed full of ideas for living with health, abundance, and compassion.

Go to www.happyliving.com to sign up for your free membership.

License Notes

Disclaimer

This book is a work of nonfiction. The events and experiences detailed herein are real and faithfully rendered to the best of the author's abilities. Some names, identities, and circumstances may have been changed to protect the privacy and anonymity of the various individuals involved.

Please note: this book and all content from Happy Living represents the personal opinions of Matt Gersper and a hand-picked team of Happy Living Experts. Before making any changes to your lifestyle, diet or exercise routines, please consult a physician or other appropriate expert.

For my parents, Paul and Freda Gersper.
You taught me to believe in myself, you supported me through every low and every high in my life, and you always love me unconditionally.

Foreword

I am truly excited for you, the reader of this book. For you, my good friend, are about to embark on a magical journey, one of transformation; the unlocking of your vast human potential. It is the discovery of what matters to you – truly and deeply – and the bringing of those treasures into your experience, to give you an incredibly rich, meaningful, joyful life.

But the journey, magical though it is, does not come cheap. Nor is it easy. You'll have to work, and you'll have to be dedicated to the outcome. "Sweat equity" is required in the beginning, as is faith in what lies on the other side of the struggle. And you'll need a healthy dose of resolve to see you through that "no man's land" between "impulse to act" and "desired result", littered, as it is, with the debris of false starts and failed attempts.

Fortunately, you have a decided advantage as you begin the next phase of your journey through life. You have Matt Gersper's book in your hands. And what Matt has laid out here for you is a blueprint for moving from impulse (inspiration) to action. And we know (if even merely at a subconscious level) that without action, all the impulse, inspiration and good intent in the world is for naught. For it is only in action, my friend, that we change our world, and benefit others too.

Or, as Tony Robbins says: Knowledge is not power... it's potential power. *Execution will trump knowledge any day.*

Aristotle, too, has weighed in on this subject with the not often enough repeated quote: *The end of science is not knowledge, but action.*

Striving to be "the change we want to see in the world" (hat tip, Mahatma Gandhi) takes great effort, no doubt. A steely resolve. Or, as the Paleo f(x) motto states: "Heal thyself, harden thyself, change the world". But know this: the biggest obstacle to creating the change you seek is YOU.

And maybe this truth has been weighing heavy on you lately. Maybe you didn't even know what it was that was making you edgy, anxious, and just plain unhappy. Maybe, just maybe, your soul's impulse (inspiration) has been thwarted by inaction. Now, that inaction may be more to do with your circumstances than your inability to self-start. Either way, Matt has written the navigational tool to see you through, over and beyond your obstacles, whatever they may be. With this book by your side, you *can* override those obstacles, whether they come from inside or outside yourself. Starting this very moment, you can begin turning your "inspiration into action"!

It is said that when the student is ready, the teacher will appear. Consider this book the vehicle, and Matt, your teacher. I wish you all the happiness in the world, and the very best of luck on your journey.

In health, fitness, and ancestral wellness –

Keith Norris
Co-Founder, Paleo f(x); the world's largest Paleo event

Table of Contents

Introduction

"You seek too much information and not enough
transformation."
(Shiri Sai Baba)

Have you ever had great ideas that never get done?
Do you get inspired and excited one day, and then
return to your same old routines the next, without
taking action on the ideas that got you so fired up?
Ever wonder why?

At conferences and gatherings of like-minded people,
it's easy to get everyone inspired about something
new. As an exhibitor, it was always a simple task for
me to get potential customers excited about a new
service. However, I used to complain that their
'enthusiasm' didn't seem to survive the trip home. I
was frustrated when they failed to take follow-up
action once they were back at work. Last year, I wrote
a post about it, How to Maximize the Benefits of Any
Conference[1].

A month after the post was published, I was invited to
speak about turning conference inspirations into
action[2]. The very thing I had just written about! To
introduce myself, I shared a simple process that I use
to make big transformations in my life. I showed the
audience how I applied the Process to athletics, to
business, to family life, to spiritual life, and even to my
love life! Then I led the workshop, showing how they

7

could apply the same process to turn conference inspirations into action upon returning home. During that workshop, a flash of inspiration hit me that sparked my transformation to become an author, leading directly to this book. I'll share more about my transformation into an author in Chapter 13.

A PROCESS FOR TRANSFORMATION

Every life is a journey of transformation. We transform from infant to child to adult. We transform from student to worker to retired citizen. Many transform from single to married to parent to grandparent. We all transform from birth to death. Transformation can be passive: It happens *to* you. Or transformation can be active: You seek it out. This book is about action. It's all about paying attention and acting on the best opportunities for your personal transformation.

The Process I have developed has led to some big transformations in my life... and taken me on a wild ride — working ten different jobs, living in more than ten houses in seven states, owning four businesses, moving cross-country four times, marrying, raising two children, divorcing, marrying again, and raising two more children. Although I never ended up exactly where I expected, each transformation has enriched my life beyond measure and has helped me become more than I was before. Each step within these transformations also revealed new opportunities, many of which I was not able to see before. That's how life is. It's constantly changing and so are we.

I seem to have a creative ability to see what everyone else sees, but have different thoughts about what I observe, and notice unique trends. When I looked back over the eight big transformations of my life, I saw a pattern that was consistent within each one. The pattern was this: There are three key questions, and three awe-inspiring "powers" that answering them unleash. Together, these questions and powers form the transformational process I've been using to create the life of my dreams.

GRAVITY

Having big ideas that never come to fruition stops you from living your absolute best life. And it's a very common problem. It's the problem when a person begins a gym membership after New Year's but then stops going by February. It's the problem when a great idea from a conference doesn't survive the trip home, and when your resolution to see a good friend every month gets postponed until it drifts back into years... Perhaps it seems like you just got too busy, or something else got in the way, or you didn't have the time, energy or budget to fulfill your idea after all. But guess what? There's a secret problem hiding behind all the "reasons" why big ideas don't come to fruition.

The *real* problem is… *Gravity*! The forces of procrastination, self-doubt, worry, cultural expectations, even family and friends, can hold your life in place, like Gravity. If they are more powerful than the forces you're using to change your life, your big ideas never get done. For example, you witness an act of kindness, reminding you of your lifelong goal to start a charitable foundation. That idea contains energy. It's a force. But it's only a weak one, like a light breeze. Gravity responds to this new force, and Gravity is more powerful. Gravity says, "How are you going to start a foundation? You don't have the money, the time, or the talent." And so your idea stalls and your life doesn't move forward. So, how do you beat Gravity?

The Answer is simple (which is not to say that the path is always easy!): Follow the Process in this book.

In Part 1, I'll discuss in detail the forces that conspire against such transformations. I'll explore many of the problems that hold you in place and prevent you from taking action. Then, I'll share the simple transformational process that I developed and implemented over the course of my life, which has worked for me, enabling me to overcome those forces. I'll discuss in detail the 3 Questions and how to apply them in your own life, and the 3 Powers they unleash to help you.

In Part 2, I'll share intimate details of the eight major transformations of my life, as examples of how the Process worked for me. Throughout the book I will also take the opportunity to share the MBG Life Lessons I have drawn from my experiences. I use my initials to highlight the fact that these are *my* life lessons and I do not presume that they should apply to you or anyone else. However, as my life lessons are essential tools which help guide me to the life of my dreams, I felt it was important to share them. I do this in the hope that they may be of use to you both in and of themselves, and to demonstrate how you can begin to draw your own life lessons from your own personal transformations too. To get us started, here is the first:

> *MBG Life Lesson:* Follow your heart wherever it leads you because it knows where your happiness lies.

In Part 3, I'll shift the focus to transforming *you*, because, at its heart, this book is about you, and my desire to help *you* make meaningful change in *your* life. My promise is to show you how to connect to the powers needed to conquer those forces which oppose change, help you act on your best opportunities, and live the life of your dreams.

Bringing change into your life changes who you are. Changing who you are then changes what you want and what you do. That, in turn, changes what you are inspired by. The process keeps repeating, over and over. It keeps you progressing in a purposeful direction with consistency. That's its secret. It will work for anyone desiring a better life, and it will work for you if you make the commitment to it.

Let's get started!

Matt Gersper

Part 1 : A Transformational Practice

Chapter 1 - Forces of Gravity

"An object at rest stays at rest and an object in motion
stays in motion with the same speed and in the same
direction unless acted upon by an unbalanced force."
(Sir Isaac Newton)

Having big ideas that never come to fruition prevents
you from living your absolute best life. It's the
problem when a person gets excited about a new diet,
and finally losing the extra weight, only to return to
their usual habits within weeks. It's also the problem
when a person dreams about becoming their own
boss but never does anything more than read inspiring
books about entrepreneurship.

The forces that are keeping your life just the way it is
are more powerful than the forces you are using to
change your life, and therefore, the changes you try to
make don't stick.

A simple physics lesson[3] illustrates this:

Let's say a notepad resting on a table represents your
life as it currently is. The notepad will not move
because the force of gravity is holding it there. It will

remain there forever unless a force greater than gravity pushes or pulls it in a different direction.

Procrastination, self-doubt, broken promises, the prevailing culture and even family and friends are forces acting like gravity to hold your life in place, just the way it is.

Your idea by itself is not powerful enough to overcome the Gravity of your life and so the notepad doesn't move. Maybe the light breeze of your idea ruffles a page or two of your life, but the gravitational pull of "what is" is so strong it keeps the notepad in place. Your new idea is just one more great inspiration that never gets done.

This is what is going on behind the scenes when you find yourself inspired and excited by an idea one day, and envision a new path, but then return to your same old self the next, changing nothing.

The gravitational forces of your life come in different shapes, sizes and voices but they are all working hard to keep your life just the way it is. Some of these forces come from inside, some come from outside, and some from an interaction of the two. Let me explain. "Inside" forces of Gravity come from a voice talking to you inside your head. Say you had an idea to start a charitable foundation, the example I used in my introduction. Here are some examples of the forces of Gravity which could stop you from moving forward with it:

Procrastination: *I'll start working on the charitable foundation after I get A, B, and C done and I have more time.* As Mark Twain famously said, "Never put off till tomorrow what you can do the day after tomorrow."

Self-doubt: *I think it would be great to run a charitable foundation but I've never done anything like that before. It's beyond my ability. I'm just kidding myself.*

Broken promises: *I started working on the charitable foundation, creating an outline of things to do and even doing some but I did not sustain my effort and eventually I just stopped.*

These inside forces of Gravity act as an internal detractor, questioning whether you deserve the change you want. They make you wonder if pursuing your goal is selfish or silly. They chip away at your confidence that the idea is achievable, and that you have the ability to achieve it. They flood your mind with negative thoughts and excuses[4].

"Outside" forces of Gravity are beliefs you have collected from your experience in the world and from your observations of it. They come from a wide variety of sources, including:

Culture: You can't start your own charitable foundation because... you are a busy mom... you do not have a college education... you are not wealthy... you do not have a resume full of executive experience. The culture we live in often sends limiting messages of what we are "supposed to do" and what we are "not supposed to do" that keep us in place, like gravity.

Family: No one in our family has ever started a charitable foundation, why do you think you can? Do you think you're better than the rest of us?

Family & Friends (Jealous): You are nothing more than an administration assistant. What makes you think you can start and run a charitable foundation?

Family & Friends (Who will miss you): I don't want you to start a charitable foundation because... you'll become too busy to spend time with me... you'll meet a new circle of friends and not have time for me... you'll develop new and different interests and won't want to spend time with me.

Some family and friends simply will not understand why you want to change your life and take on new challenges. They are more comfortable with you just like you are. They may see something in your changes that they desire for themselves. They may fear losing you. Whatever the case, these outside forces of Gravity can weigh heavily on you. Some Gravity that works to prevent you from changing your life comes from an interaction between "inside" and "outside" forces, as in the examples that follow:

Information Overload: The massive volume of time-demand responding to email, text messages, social media messages, news feeds and other non-critical "time sucks" creates a feeling of busyness that can provide a continuous excuse for the procrastinator inside your head.

Blaming (Others): I would have started working on the charitable foundation except the consultant I hired said I didn't have... enough money... enough experience... enough support. This outside voice feeds the self-doubt inside your head.

Blaming (Things): I would have started working on the charitable foundation except... My boss just assigned me a big project... The kids just started back to school... Another company just started something similar to my idea. These outside events strengthen the forces of Gravity inside your head.

Remember our physics lesson: An object at rest stays at rest unless acted upon by an unbalanced force.

Your life as it is today is like the object at rest. There are powerful gravitational forces working very hard to keep it just as it is. If you want to change it, you need to use forces greater than Gravity to push or pull it in a different direction. You need a pathway to greater power.

Chapter 2 - A Pathway to Greater Power

"Go forth, giving thought to what you are wanting, attracting life experience to help you decide what you want, and once you have decided, giving thought only onto that.[5]"
(Abraham Hicks)

There are two distinct pathways people take to create big changes in their life. These are inspiration and devastation.

Have you noticed how some people seem to tap into a deeper power in response to a disaster? Here are three examples, from three very different people, who have overcome incredible calamities by drawing on some deep, inner power. They each inspire me to be a better person.

Viktor Frankl[6] witnessed and endured unfathomable atrocities during three years in three different concentration camps during World War II. His wife Tilly, mother Elsa, father Gabriel, and brother Walter all died or were killed during their captivity. Apart from himself, the only survivor of the Holocaust among Frankl's immediate relatives was his sister Stella. Somehow, through all the horror, Viktor was able to identify a purpose in his current circumstances to feel positively about, and then center his focus on that.

On April 27, 1945, the Americans liberated him. In 1946, he wrote a book about his experiences as a German prisoner, and described the method he used to survive. *Man's Search for Meaning*[7] is one of the ten most influential books in the United States[8]. It is an important book for everyone to read.

Jennifer Bricker was born without legs and given up for adoption at birth. Fortunately, wonderful parents who viewed her condition as an opportunity, not a disability, adopted her. Sharon and Gerald Bricker had one simple rule in their family: never say the word "can't". They applied this rule equally to their three "able-bodied" sons and their adopted daughter.

Their rule worked wonders. Jennifer says, "If you are never given limits, then you think, 'I can do anything'." She took this attitude all the way to the top of her sport, becoming the tumbling champion for the state of Illinois. This video clip[9], originally part of HBO's *Real Sports with Bryant Gumbel*, reports that Jennifer is now in Hollywood, living an independent life and earning a living as a gymnast.

Bethany Hamilton survived a 2003 shark attack in which her left arm was bitten off. An article from www.home-school.com reports:

While still lying in bed, with her arm recently bandaged, 13-year-old Bethany was smiling at visitors and quietly pondering her future. She had always wanted to be a professional surfer, but would it be possible to surf at all with just one arm? And would she have the courage to go back in the water again? The answer to the second question was a big fat "Yes!" A surfer since before she could walk, Bethany determined to surf again if she possibly could. She would just trust God for the outcome, as she had been doing all along[10].

Bethany has an indomitable spirit. She says, "It's almost nice that it happened when I was young," because it was easier for her to adapt to the change. Sounds like she lost her favorite surfboard, not her left arm! I smiled the entire time watching this short video, How Does She Do It | One Arm Surf Girl[11].

Imagine the incredible pull Gravity must have had on Viktor, Jennifer, and Bethany, given the horrendous conditions thrust upon them. They had every excuse to give in to the circumstances of their lives, but they did not. From their stories comes a lesson: When faced with devastating obstacles, human beings are able to access an inner strength that is astonishing. I have great admiration for every person who finds a hidden strength, from deep within, to not only survive but to somehow thrive when life thrusts disaster upon them. I hope these three examples of tremendous courage and spirit in the face of calamity will inspire you, too.

Thankfully, my pathway to power has been inspiration, not devastation. The remainder of this book will focus on using inspiration as the pathway to greater levels of power. In the introduction, I shared how a flash of inspiration hit me while speaking to conference delegates and sparked my transformation to become an author. Now I will explain how I take that initial inspiration and harness the 3 Powers: the Power of Priority, the Power of the Heart and the Power of the Universe, so that I can overcome Gravity and really start making things happen.

THREE QUESTIONS, THREE POWERS

When inspiration strikes, I use a process based on 3 Questions to begin exploring the potential transformation. Each question has the ability to activate and leverage a greater level of power. This power then becomes available to me to use in the process of turning my inspirations into action. The 3 Questions are WHAT? WHY? and HOW?, and the 3 Powers these questions unleash are the Power of Priority, the Power of the Heart and the Power of the Universe. These 3 Powers have the strength to overcome the Gravity which keeps me from making big changes in my life. In the following chapters, I will discuss the 3 Questions and the 3 Powers in depth, and show you how to apply it to your inspirations.

KAIZEN

Before I get to the three questions, it's important that you have an understanding of a concept called Kaizen. Kaizen is the Japanese idea that small, incremental improvements will add up over time to yield big results. As a personal practice, it means that there is always something you can do better tomorrow than you did today. It keeps you moving forward. Every single day. You may choose to work on a craft, or a physical skill, or a spiritual practice. You could be expanding your capacity for kindness, or becoming a better listener, or tolerating others more graciously. Kaizen can be applied to anything that you want to do better. Kaizen greases your willingness to say YES and try new things on your pathway to greater power.

Chapter 3 - Question 1: 'WHAT?'

"The law of attraction is this: You don't attract what
you want. You attract what you are."
(Dr. Wayne W. Dyer)

Let's begin with the first question, WHAT?

Asking *"WHAT inspires me?"* is the process of
exploring ideas that could take you on the journey to
the life of your dreams. This question is based on the
Law of Attraction. I believe each of us have unique
interests, and talents, and purposes for being on this
planet. For example, I am interested in writing books.
You may be interested in writing songs. I am
interested in hiking and paddle boarding. You may be
interested in gardening. I am interested in how
meditation and sleep help support brain health. You
may be interested in how political turmoil in one
country affects the financial markets in another.

WHAT you are interested in is very important. It's the
first step to accessing enough power to overcome
Gravity and move your life in the direction you
choose.

The process of asking and answering this first question
is like brainstorming for big ideas. Your work is to sift
through ideas looking for golden nuggets that will help

you on your journey to your absolute best life. It requires paying attention to what attracts you. It's how you prepare yourself so that inspiration comes to you like a lightning bolt.

The process of asking WHAT you are wanting is not the moment for judging and then either accepting or rejecting ideas that come to you. It is about allowing ideas to flow to you. It is the time for gathering as much information as possible about what you are attracted to.

I prepare myself to receive inspiration with relaxation, connection, exploration, and reflection. My mind relaxes when my body is engaged in activities I enjoy. I reach a state of mental relaxation by doing simple activities like hiking, paddle boarding, and showering. I have had many "Aha!" moments this way. In fact, when I am struggling with an issue and can't find a solution, I'll make it the theme of a hike or other enjoyable activity. This is a soft mental action. For example, I may be focusing on an important task at work and come to a cross road with two very different options, where the decision is mine to make. I'll prepare my mind by thinking through the facts and options, and then try to relax during my exercise, not consciously thinking about the issue. Often times, in that open, easy, receptive mode, an idea or option just comes to me. My work here it to reach this relaxed state of mind by focusing on the physical activity I am engaged in, rather than to 'resolve the issue'. With a relaxed and clear mind, I am preparing myself for ideas and inspirations to flow to me and a resolution naturally becomes apparent.

Connecting with other people is another way in which I gather ideas and inspiration. When I was in high school, I was inspired at football camps. I remember meeting Fred Biletnikoff[12] and thinking how 'normal' he looked. He wasn't very big. He wasn't very fast. He even smoked cigarettes. Seeing him in person allowed me to believe I could make it to the pros. I'll have more on how Fred Biletnikoff inspired me in Chapter 6.

As an adult, industry conferences have been a great source of ideas and inspiration for me. Traveling to a conference takes me out of my regular routine, focuses me on the process of learning, and introduces me to many new people and ideas. All of these things prepare my mind for inspiration to strike. Visiting with family and friends is another way I relax my mind, and I enjoy working through new ideas in conversation. My work when connecting with other people is to be curious, listen more than I talk, and pay attention to what captures my interest.

I also really love to explore, in all kinds of ways. Exploration exposes me to different places, new experiences, and fresh ideas. My most frequent type of exploration is reading. I make it a practice to read every day, and I am usually reading several books at once. Reading lets me see the world through the eyes of others. It provides me with new ways of thinking, and it helps bring structure to my own ideas and thoughts. Traveling lets me see the world with my own eyes. It benefits me by breaking my routine, relaxing my mind with pleasant activity, and enriching my life with real experiences. When I travel, I am more aware, more in the "now", focused on the moment. Exploring new places, learning about different cultures, eating different foods, trying new things, and living in the moment floods the mind with opportunities for inspiration. Movies, documentaries, and TV shows are another way I explore other places, get exposure to other people and their way of thinking, and learn new things that may inspire me.

REFLECTION

I have a rather strong practice of reflection, which I find to be a powerful tool for allowing inspiration to strike. Birthdays, the New Year and other milestones cause me to pause and reflect on where I am, where I've been, and where I'm going. I have used New Year's resolutions as a catalyst for self-improvement for most of my life. Reflection has been such a great tool for me that I've added a few routines that help keep me prepared for inspiration to strike. I offer them to you here in the hope that they may inspire you to create your own.

Firstly, I have a weekly routine I call *Coffee, Classical, and Priority*. On Monday mornings I sit down with a cup of coffee, turn on classical music, and reflect on what has real value and deep meaning for me. I spend an hour focusing on the major priorities of my life, reviewing how I spent time the previous week, and making sure my calendar in the coming week is aligned with those things that I most care about.

Secondly, once a month, I schedule one day for *Thinking and Planning*. I try to keep this day free from any work or personal obligations. It's my time to be quiet, relax my mind and pay attention. The practice of reflection taps a relaxed but focused mental energy that helps me challenge my current life, consider new options, and give thought to what I am attracted to. It has been a great source for discovering WHAT I want for my life. Interestingly, reflection also helps me do the work of Question 2 and determine WHY I want it.

Chapter 4 - Question 2: 'WHY?'

"Sometimes the heart sees what is invisible to the eyes."
(H. Jackson Brown Jr.)

Once we have the WHAT, we can ask the second question: *WHY is it important to you?* Asking WHY is the process of choosing the things that touch your heart. This is how you create a prioritized life.

I define spirituality as discovering and cultivating the inner being that is my unique soul. It is a practice of awareness. It is noticing whether energy is coming from my mind or is generated from deep within my soul. Through my practice of reflection (slowing down, being quiet, and listening for my heart to show me the way), I created *The Seven Wonders of My Life*, which act as my filters and allow me to compare any new inspiration against what's fundamentally important to me. I offer them here in the hope that they will inspire you to name and cherish the wonders in your life, too. My Seven Wonders are:

> 1. *My one true love*: being a loving and devoted husband.

> 2. *My family*: providing love, support, and leadership.

3. *My friends*: connecting and celebrating life together.

4. *Fitness*: caring for my body, mind, and spirit.

5. *Finance*: investing in charities, businesses, and people doing good work.

6. *Adventure*: exploring different places, new experiences, and fresh ideas.

7. *Business*: researching, experimenting, and writing about best practices for Happy Living.

The Seven Wonders of My Life are my filters for deciding what is important to me and what is not. As I mentioned in the introduction, when an idea strikes, I use my filters to choose what matters to me and eliminate everything else. This helps me say YES to ideas, opportunities, and inspirations that are in alignment with my heart and to quickly say NO to everything else. By eliminating things that are not important to me, I make space for those that are. The more I say "No" to what I don't want, the more time, energy and resources I have for what matters most to me. This is the Power of Priority.

ANCHORING

The second Power, the Power of the Heart, comes from anchoring.

Filtering says, "This is in, and this is out." Anchoring answers the question of WHY?

Exploring and answering the question WHY is the key to unlocking the Power of the Heart. WHY is the process of choosing the things from the treasure trove of ideas, opportunities and inspirations that asking WHAT has brought me. Knowing WHY is so critical that my daughter and I wrote an entire book about it, called The Belief Road Map[13]. Asking WHY guides me to choose only the inspirations that touch my heart. It's the process of determining what is not only attractive to me, but also important. I know the things that are most important to me because they are in alignment with who I am, in my heart.

Knowing WHY something is important to me gives me the power and energy to overcome the powerful forces of "Gravity" holding my life in place. Understanding WHY is the key to unleashing the Power of the Heart.

To answer the question WHY, I access the inner being that is my unique soul. I've learned to detect the differences between energy and ideas created by my mind and those generated deep within my heart. The mind is held down by forces of Gravity: Procrastination, blame, self-doubt, what others say and think, cultural issues, etc. The heart is lifted by things that have great importance to your true self. When you feel your heart soar at an idea, or feel joy bubble up from deep within you about an opportunity... when it just deep down feels good, you know it has importance to you, and that feeling is a key to unleashing the Power of the Heart.

When I explored WHY in relation to my idea of writing this book, for example, I discovered that it touched on my heartstrings, my business-strings, my financial-strings, even my personal-strings. It was anchored to who I am and what I want. I was hooked!

In the pursuit of happiness it's the journey that matters most because the destination (what I want) keeps moving. Who I am and what I want is constantly evolving. A quote by Heraclitus, a pre-Socratic Greek philosopher, says, "No man ever steps in the same river twice, for it's not the same river and he's not the same man."

That's how life is. It is changing and we are changing.

Peter Drucker, the Austrian-born American management consultant, educator, and author, once said, "Efficiency is doing things right, effectiveness is doing the right things."

> *MBG Life Lesson*: Efficiency is doing things right, effectiveness is doing the right things.

Reflection and filtering help me choose the right things for my best life.

COMMIT TO ASKING WHAT? AND WHY?

I make a constant practice of paying attention to WHAT I am attracted to, and WHY. Doing so keeps me evolving in a positive direction, creating a life based on who I am and what I want. WHAT is possible for me today is very different from what was possible twenty years ago. So many things have changed in the world – some for the better and some for the worse. The same can be said about me. So many things have changed within me and my life compared to twenty years ago – some for the better and some for the worse.

> *MBG Life Lesson*: All of you are perfect just as you are and you could use a little improvement.

This Life Lesson is a direct quote from Shunryu Suzuki-roshi, a Sōtō Zen monk and teacher who helped popularize Zen Buddhism in the United States[14], and it serves as a guiding principle for continuous improvement in my life.

I believe each day is an opportunity to make change for the better. The constant nature of change creates opportunity for those who keep looking. I am constantly looking, and I pay attention when an inspiration moves me. That's my heart leading me to even greater happiness.

Creating positive change is hard. As we have discovered, there are many forces at work to hold a life in place. Prioritizing my life around what's most important to me, and anchoring changes to who I am and what I want creates the power, energy, and time I need to overcome the forces of Gravity in my life.

Asking WHY? is the key to unleashing the Power of Priority and the Power of the Heart.

In the next step, which is figuring out HOW to make real changes in life, I'll begin to demonstrate how I use Power of Priority and Power of the Heart and I'll be exploring the third power, Power of the Universe.

Chapter 5 - Question 3: 'HOW?'

"It is good to have an end to journey toward; but it is the journey that matters, in the end."
(Ernest Hemingway)

The Power of Priority and the Power of the Heart both create energy that can be used to change your life. The Power of the Universe provides even more energy and other support when you actually begin *doing the work*.

You've given yourself the freedom to discover WHAT you want. You've reflected on WHY it is important to you, and you've anchored the change to the things that hold the most importance in your life. Now is the time to make the firm commitment to change. In order to change your life, you must change who you are and what you do. You need to make the commitment to go the distance. Change can be hard. Change requires more energy, more focus, more time, and more resources than remaining as you are. You must be prepared to endure a rough road on the way to your better life. But don't be discouraged - when you anchor an idea, an opportunity, or an inspiration to what is truly important to you, deep within your spirit, the 3 Powers will provide the energy to sustain the change.

A quote from Confucius helps me keep the challenging nature of change in perspective: "It does not matter how slowly you go as long as you do not stop." I have taken this as a Life Lesson.

> *MBG Life Lesson*: It does not matter how slowly you go as long as you do not stop.

Are you familiar with the term "Burn the boats?" Here's the story from BurningBoats.com[15].

> It was the year 1519 and Hernán Cortés, with some 600 Spaniards, 16 or so horses and 11 boats, had landed on a vast inland plateau called, Mexico.
>
> The Spanish conquistador and his men were about to embark on a conquest of an empire that hoarded some of the world's greatest treasure. Gold, silver and precious Aztec jewels were just some of what this treasure had to offer anyone who succeeded in their quest to obtain it.
>
> But, with only 600 men — none of whom had encumbered themselves with protective armor — conquering an empire so extensive in its territories could only be undertaken by a man with a death wish.

This daring undertaking was made even more insurmountable by the fact that for more than 600 years, conquerors with far more resources at their disposal who attempted to colonize the Yucatan Peninsula, never succeeded. Hernán Cortés was well-aware of this fact. And it was for this reason, that he took a different approach when he landed on the land of the Mayans.

Instead of charging through cities and forcing his men into immediate battle, Hernán Cortés stayed on the beach and awoke the souls of his men with melodious cadences – in the form of emblazoned speeches. His speeches were ingeniously designed to urge on the spirit of adventure and invoke the thirst of lifetimes of fortune amongst his troops. His orations bore fruit, for what was supposedly a military exploit, now bore the appearance of extravagant romance in the imaginations of Cortés' troops.

But, ironically, it would only just be 3 words which Cortés' murmured, that would change the history of the New World. As they marched inland to face their enemies, Cortés ordered, "**Burn the boats**."

It was a decision that should have back-fired. For if Cortés and his men were on the brink of defeat, there wasn't an exit strategy in place to save their lives. Remarkably though, the command to burn the boats had an opposite effect on his men because now, they were left with only 2 choices — die, or ensure victory. And fight they did.

We know today, how Cortés' decision to burn his boats panned out. Hernán Cortés became the first man in 600 years to successfully conquer Mexico.

That's the point. You have made a thoughtful decision to change something very important in your life, so you do not stop. There is no going back. In fact, it's time to "burn the boats" so you cannot return to your previous life. You are ready to do this because the change you want deeply touches your heart.

It's time to figure out HOW you will bring the change into your life.

That's something only you can decide on. To help you, I'd like to share my experience of what works for me. There are four areas I concentrate on when I have decided to make a big change in my life: time, routines, resources and focus.

TIME

So, I've decided I want to do something more with my life. I am ready to transform myself into something more. But there are still only twenty-four hours in a day and suddenly there is more I want to do. This first thing I do is determine the specific things I need to do to bring about the change, and how much time each will take. When I made the final decision to write this book, I decided that I was going to dedicate ninety minutes a day, five days a week to the book project. The project included all the planning and the actual writing, but also all the steps involved in publishing and marketing a book. I created a list with more than thirty different action items to be completed. I used this list as my guide. I checked off items after completing them, added to the list as I learned something new, and re-prioritized the order of things to do as required.

The next thing I did was decide what I was going to give up. I've learned if I don't give something up (at least equal in time commitment), I will not find the time I need to create the change I want. I decided to give up all the product development work I was doing for Happy Living. During our first year in business, we were working on developing proprietary software and products, and hosting retreats to teach our Seven Foundations of Health. The idea for this book, and the greater inspiration of becoming an author, fit me so perfectly that I just *had* to make space for it. Creating that space meant making some tough decisions, too. In this case, it meant giving up on some projects I was very attached to. The fact that I made the choice to give them up and understood why I was doing so made it easier, though. And the knowledge that I was giving those projects up in order to ensure that my exciting new dream really would come to fruition gave me the strength to let go of them. You may also find, as I have, that when you step back from something in this way, you create an opportunity for someone else to step in and fulfill the next part of his or her current dream or journey, too.

ROUTINES

Routines and habits are what keep my life in order. I've read that it takes twenty-one days to form a habit, and in my own life I've found that the more I do something, the easier it gets to keep doing it. And at some point, it becomes automatic. So when I am ready to transform myself into something more, I re-order the routines in my life, and build new habits to support the change I am after.

For example, before I made the decision to write this book, my workday routine looked something like this: 6:40-wake, 7:00-read, 8:00-work, 2:30-exercise, 4:30-cook dinner/family time. After my decision, my workday routine looked like this: 6:40-wake, 7:00-meditate, 7:30-write, 9:00-stretch, 9:15-read, 10:00-work, 2:30-exercise, 4:30-cook dinner/family time. I not only made space for my writing project but I put it at the beginning of the day to give it maximum priority. You'll also notice that I took advantage of this re-ordering of my life to add two additional things that I had been wanting to do more consistently: meditation and stretching. Simply "saying" I want something is easy and comes from my head. "Doing the work" of what I most care about is aligned with my heart. I believe you can tell what someone *actually* cares about by looking at how they *actually* spend their time. Just looking at my new schedule brought me joy because it reflected the reality that I was becoming an author.

RESOURCES

When I'm ready to make a big change in my life, I look for opportunities to use the resources at my disposal to support the change. Time may be the most valuable one but there are others, such as money, connections, libraries, schools, the Internet, service providers, and even social pressure.

For example, as part of my transformation into an author, I used the Internet to conduct research on writing and publishing. I also bought a book on self-publishing, and I invested time and money in a self-publishing school[16]. I sought out advice by connecting with people who have written books or who knew people who had. I used our platform at Happy Living and social media resources such as Facebook, Twitter,

LinkedIn, Google+, and Pinterest to promote the book. Promoting the book had the added advantage of creating social pressure as I publically announced my decision to write it before even putting the first word on a page.

FOCUS

A firm decision to bring a big change into your life brings with it a change in focus. The decision itself changes how you see the world, and what you see in it. For example, in my 20's, I worked in several businesses that sold sprinkler systems to homeowners. I became somewhat of an expert on drip-irrigation systems. If I visited your home during that time of my life, I would notice everything about your irrigation system. It was important to me, and I brought it into my world everywhere I went through my attention.

Also, during my time running an international trade company, I would notice shipping containers everywhere. When I was driving on the highway, I'd see them on trucks or trains. When traveling by air, I'd spot them at the airports. When visiting coastal cities, I'd observe that the seaports were chock-full of containers. Just seeing them brought me joy because they were a symbol of something very important to me during that time of my life. I brought them into my world through my attention. My decision to become an author has completely changed the world I see, once again.

Now that we have explored the forces that can hold a life in place and the 3 Powers that can be used to create change, I am ready to share with you how I have used the Process in my own life. I feel it is important to provide intimate details of my personal transformations as examples of how the Process worked for me, so you can see it in action and begin to imagine using it in your life.

THE POWER TO TRANSFORM

Before moving on, I'd like to share this observation. The Process is all about increasing your power to transform your life, not reducing the forces of Gravity holding it in place. It's an important distinction. The forces of procrastination, self-doubt, worry, cultural expectations, family and friends, etc. exist. They are real forces. Many of them are out of your control. We are not going to waste any valuable energy trying to reduce their gravitational pull. Instead, we'll be exploring how to apply the 3 Questions in your own life such that you unleash the 3 Powers to overwhelm the forces of Gravity. Think of it this way. Michael Jordan, perhaps the greatest basketball player in history, experienced precisely the same pull from Earth's gravitational force as every other player. However, he trained so hard and became so powerful, he seemed to literally defy gravity as he made spectacular, high-flying plays. That's what I want the

Process to do for you, make it seem like you defy Gravity as you connect to the powers you need to conquer negativity, act on the best opportunities, and live the life of your dreams.

For now, let's dive into the eight major transformations of my life.

PART 2: Transforming Me

Bringing new and interesting ideas into my life keeps changing who I am. Changing who I am then changes what I want and what I do. That, in turn, changes what I am attracted to. The transformational Process keeps repeating, over and over.

It is a virtuous cycle paving the way to the life of my dreams.

I believe that is my personal responsibility to continuously create a better me if I want a better life. That's why I have made a firm commitment to continuous change and improvement by using the practice of reflection and the 3 Questions. I make a constant practice of paying attention to WHAT I am attracted to, which is my Pathway to Power. Filters help me activate the Power of Priority. Understanding WHY something's important to me unleashes the Power of the Heart. When I figure out HOW I'll bring the change into my life and begin doing the work, I invoke the Power of the Universe, which picks up the path with me and runs with it, yielding fresh energy, insights and connections to aid me at every turn. My commitment to embracing continuous transformation has taken me on a wild journey to my absolute best life.

As you'll soon see, this Process has resulted in a lot of twists and turns along the way! In the following chapters, I'm going to share my journey to becoming the expanded, transformed me that I am here and now. It is my sincere wish that every transformation along the way resonates with your own journey in some way, and that, looking at my personal path of transformation as a whole, you can draw some helpful insights to assist you on your own transformational path.

.

Chapter 6 - Pro Football
(1975 – 1985)

"Once you get where you want to be, you're not there
anymore."
(Unknown)

I was lying on the grass, stretching with my group of
defensive backs. It was July 1984 in El Segundo,
California. We were warming up for another morning
practice. The previous day had been a very good one
for me. I had two highlights. First, Mr. Al Davis, the
General Manager of the team, was walking the
sidelines, watching and observing, taking everything
in. As he walked passed me, he said, "How's it going,
Matt?" "Great Mr. Davis," I replied, "Everything is
going great." I was surprised. I was an undrafted,
Division II Strong Safety out of U.C. Davis. I had tried
out for the Saskatchewan Roughriders, in the
Canadian Football League, and had been cut within a
week. Shortly after being released by the Roughriders,
I got a workout at a local junior college with Axel
Schmidt, a scout for the Raiders. He was the father of
a friend of mine who played tight end during my time
at Davis. The workout went well. Mr. Schmidt
recommended the Raiders sign me to a contract. It
was very exciting signing on with the World Champion
Los Angeles Raiders. They had just won the Super
Bowl, beating the Washington Redskins, 38 to 9.

When Al Davis called me by name and asked how I was doing, I figured that this man must know every single detail about his organization. "I'm a nobody," I thought, "from a small school, just cut from a 2nd tier league, and he knows who I am."

The second highlight for me came during a play in practice. In high school and college, I had developed a reputation for being a big hitter. Making a big hit was my favorite part of the game. I looked for opportunities and developed specific techniques that made my hitting more impactful. That day in El Segundo, I got to bring eight years' worth of practice, training, eating to gain weight, skipping vacations, waking early to run, and developing the art of hitting to a mountain of a man. He was a 6'6", 305-pound right guard the Raider's had drafted the year before. I was playing Strong Safety. The center snapped the ball. The tight end blocked down meaning the run was coming my way. I exploded to my gap hoping to meet the ball carrier but expecting a pulling guard. I readied my 6'3, 195-pound body to take on this 305-pound monster. I hit him with every bit of power I could muster. And I hit him on his left side, when his legs were extended, one foot in front of the other; right at the moment when his body was most unstable. And the big man fell! My hit jammed up the entire play and we held the runner to no gain. What a great feeling!

So, picture the scene. The following morning, we're halfway through our stretches, and Art Shell, who was the offensive line coach at the time, is walking towards my group with a big black player. He motions towards Willie Brown, who was my defensive back coach. They appeared to be negotiating for a trade. It turned out that there was only one black player on the offensive line, and I was the only white player in the defensive backfield. Art was telling Willie, if he agreed to the trade, we'd be more color coordinated. It was a funny moment but I wasn't with the Raiders for fun. I didn't care about big pulling guards, or Al Davis, or about being in a practical joke between Hall-of-Famers. I didn't care that I was considered a nobody in NFL terms. I knew I could play. I knew I could hit. I knew I had trained for eight long years to be right here. Right now. I was very focused. This was the chance of my lifetime. In just a few months, the Los Angeles Raiders would begin the regular season in Houston, against the Oilers. And I expected to be there.

A BOY WITH A DREAM

When I was in the fifth grade at Parkmead Elementary, my teacher Mrs. Roth assigned a six-chapter autobiography. The final chapter was "The Future".

I wrote:

I plan to go to High School. There I will work on science and history mainly. I will try out for the football and basketball teams. Maybe I will get a scholarship. Then I will go to Ohio State University, get a job, and try out for the football team. It will take a lot to make it. If I do, I will be able to go to a pro team, hopefully the Cincinnati Bengals. Get married, and have three kids, and live on Tick Ridge (in southern Ohio). I want to play for ten years and then sit back and take it easy. If I don't get on a football team, I'll have a lot of thinking to do.

Four years later, I was on a small plateau about a quarter mile from Del Valle High School in Walnut Creek, California. It held the football field, an unmarked practice field, a small set of bleachers on one side, a dirt track around the football field, and a small storage building called the Quonset[17] hut. I would soon be spending a lot of time there. Four years of football practices. Four years of track and field. And four years out there by myself, training my body outside of organized practices.

I was 5' 2" and 100 pounds when I started high school. To compete in athletics, I always had to work harder than other boys who were naturally bigger, stronger and faster than me. So the first day of freshman football practice was not my first day on that field. I had been there all summer long. Running laps. Running routes. Preparing for this moment.

50

The head varsity football coach was the father of one of my best friends. He had shared with me his summer aerobic and strength training for his players. I followed every recommendation, and did even more. I was in the best shape of my life. I was focused. I was fit. I was eager. In short, I was ready!

I had wanted to play tackle football for as long as I could remember but I was always too small to play on the Pop Warner teams in my area. I had played flag football every year since the fourth grade. But this day, I was in full-gear for the first time in my life.

It was exciting. Putting on football gear was always a transformative process for me. The slow deliberate ritual of pulling on snuggly fitted, padded pants, shoulder pads, forearm pads, the football jersey, and lacing up the cleats armored my body, turning me into a highly-trained weapon. Oh, but putting on my helmet changed who I was. The polite, nice Matt stayed in the locker room. A football warrior took the field ready to inflict pain on the opponent, or anyone else who stood in his way.

I'd have to wait for my first hit, though.

The coaches were getting their first look at the thirty or so boys who showed up for freshman football tryouts. Some of the boys had experience but many, like me, had never played tackle football. The coaches ran us. They put us through drills. They organized us in position groups and began teaching us how to become a football team. But that first day, there was no contact.

I'd have to wait even longer for my first hit.

At the end of practice, the coaches separated us into three teams: A, B, and C.

At home, after my first day of high school, my mom asked about my day. I stood in the doorway between our kitchen and hallway. I was humiliated. I was angry. I slid slowly down the wall until I was sitting on floor. I looked up at her. Tears of pure frustration welled up in my eyes.

"I am on the C team," I announced.

I was crushed, yes, but I was determined, too. I would have another opportunity to show what I could do. And I would do better.

BIG JACK

I remember my first full contact with Jack Holliday. I was playing left Cornerback, on the B team (yes, my determination had paid off and I'd been promoted). The A team was on offense and the man-child, Jack Holliday, was at Fullback. I didn't know Jack. He had gone to a different intermediate school like many others on the team. I didn't know what to think of him when I first saw him, either. He was about 5' 10" tall, 160 pounds. He was lean and muscular. He had sideburns. He was a *man*! And yet, somehow, impossibly, he was a high school freshman, like me!

The Quarterback yelled, the Center snapped the ball, faked a pitch to the Halfback running to the right side, and handed it to Jack. Jack ran straight through the '2' gap, next to the Center on the right side. Not only was he big, but Jack was also fast, and one of the toughest players on the team. I recognized the play. I started running as fast as I could toward where Jack would be. I had the perfect bead on him.

I was fearless. I accelerated as I prepared for the collision. I hit Jack with every bit of power I could muster. And I bounced right off him. I don't think he broke stride, or even noticed me, as he sprinted towards a touchdown.

I was humbled and embarrassed but I knew that tomorrow was another day. If I were going to make it in football, I'd have to figure out how to tackle guys like Jack Holliday.

NOT SO FAST FREDDY

As a small player, I faced many obstacles on the rocky road to pro football. Through every low, and every high, my parents supported me, one hundred percent. They taught me to believe I could accomplish anything

I set my mind to if I was willing to work long enough and hard enough for it.

One of the best things they did for my football career was to pay for me to attend football camps all through high school. We were a family rich in many ways, but money was not one of them. On a very tight household budget, they made sacrifices so that I could pursue my dream. These camps helped my physical development as a football player. They taught me new skills, provided a higher level of competition, and gave me an extra week of practice leading into each season. But the most important thing these camps did for me was to expose me to professional athletes. Seeing these pro football players in person demystified the whole idea of "pro football". These were mortal, human beings, playing the sport I loved, and they were getting paid to do it.

One player in particular helped me believe I could do it too!

I met Fred Biletnikoff the summer of my junior year. He was the outstanding wide receiver for the Oakland Raiders. The year before, he was named Most Valuable Player of Super Bowl XI, after the Raiders 32 to 14 whooping of the Minnesota Vikings. Ten years later, he would be inducted into the NFL Hall of Fame. I remember thinking how "normal" he looked. He wasn't very big (6' 1", 190 pounds) and wasn't very fast (earning him the nickname "Not So Fast Freddy"[17]). He even smoked cigarettes!

> *Lightning Bolt:* Seeing Fred Biletnikoff in person gave me the confidence to believe I could make it to the pros. That belief added fuel to my intense focus and effort to transform myself into a professional football player.

DREAM KILLERS

On the back patio of our home in Walnut Creek, my mom and dad were having an intense discussion with long-time family friends. We had lived next door to them during my early elementary school days. Our families' bond had grown through the years. The parents had watched each other's kids grow up. Our friendship had a familial feel to it. We were close. We looked out for each other. We loved each other.

It was love that brought them to our patio to have a very difficult discussion with my parents. They had observed over the years how my mom and dad supported my dream to become a pro football player. They knew my parents "spent money they didn't have" to support my football camps. They had heard them tell me, a thousand times, I could become anything I wanted, if I "was willing to work long enough and hard enough for it".

When I was a little boy, my parents' friends had thought my football dream was cute. I was a junior in high school now. It wasn't cute anymore. They "knew" that I wasn't going to become a professional football player and thought my parents had better sit me down and set me straight. And they felt that if my parents didn't do this, they were setting me up for a big failure.

It took a lot of courage for them to take this stand with my parents. It risked their friendship. They did it because they believed every word they said, and because they loved me and wanted me to have every opportunity for a successful life. They weren't alone in their opinion, either. My dream to become a pro football player typically received one of two responses from those around me; either it was dismissed as the fanciful dream of a little boy, or derided as a wasteful fantasy for a middle-class, educated young man who should become well-rounded, and should be pursuing more realistic goals. My parents accepted their advice as well intentioned but it didn't change their mind or behavior. Fortunately, the friendship survived.

How many dreams are killed before they even get started? How many inspirations are tamped down because the tampers don't understand the dreamers? How many great lives are made average by choosing or being forced onto a safer, more realistic path? I didn't have many assets on my difficult journey to becoming a professional football player, but the two biggest ones I had were:

Heart: I wanted it deep down inside me. I was willing to do almost anything.

Belief: I really, truly, believed I could do it.

Several factors helped me believe.

I have already mentioned the huge impact Fred Biletnikoff made on me. That was the first.

Secondly, some people have a sense of who they are and what they are going to be. Even from very early in their life, they seem to be uninterested and unmoved by the opinions of other people. Dr. Wayne W. Dyer[19] called people like this, "Scurvy elephants". He said he grew up having a knowing inside of him about how to do things and how he was going to live his life. And how to make things happen. And how not to be worried about what everybody else thinks of you. He said, "I came in with that. I just seem to have a knowing about that." Wayne Dyer was one of these people, and so was I. Somehow, I just had a sense that I was to become a professional football player.

Number three, my parents always believed in me. They never doubted me. They always encouraged me. They taught me that I could accomplish anything I set my mind to if I was willing to work long enough and hard enough for it. It was very simple for me. I wanted to become a professional football player and I believed I could do it.

KNOCKED OUT, COLD

I recognized the horrible, toxic fumes entering through my nose as I breathed in. I had been knocked unconscious during a practice earlier in the season, too. That was the first time I had been revived by smelling salts. It had taken a few days before my memory fully recovered.

This time was different. I slowly regained consciousness lying on grass, under the stadium lights. My coach was asking me questions. Players were looking down at me. I began to remember. I was at Acalanes High School. It was the opening kick off. I had hit the ball carrier hard, with the left side of my helmet squarely in his chest. At the same time, I'd taken a heavy blow from his teammate on the right side of *my* chest. My body had spun around and I was knocked out cold.

After I was revived, the coach put me back in the game. I felt like I was sleepwalking. I was playing in a fog. I had lost my memory. Our Quarterback, Rob Tracewell, would call the play in the huddle for all the players, and then tell me separately what my assignment was because I couldn't remember. I would carry out his instructions and we'd huddle again.

The only clear memory I have of that entire night was of something that happened during halftime. My mind was still hazy as I sat next to our Running Back, Brian Michelson, and we had this surreal conversation.

Me: "What's the score?"

Brian: "21 – 0."

Me: "Who's winning?"

Brian: "We are."

Me: "Who scored?"

Brian: "I scored two, and you scored one."

Me: "Oh, that's good."

It's a sad fact that I only scored two touchdowns that entire year and I can't remember one of them.

In his New York Times Bestseller, *Concussion*, Dr. Bennet Omalu is shining a bright light on the dangerous, long-term consequences of concussions. In 2002, he discovered a disease, called chronic traumatic encephalopathy (commonly known as CTE) caused by blows to the head that could affect everyone playing the game of football. In 1979, the health risks of two concussions never entered my foggy mind, even after it cleared. My road to professional football was going to be a bumpy one, and these were just some of the bumps.

REJECTION & BROKEN PROMISES

One night, shortly after my final season of high school football, my parents and I were anxiously awaiting a dinner guest. When he arrived, Jim Sochor was not what I expected. He was a small man, with a soft voice, and he spoke more like a university professor than a head football coach. After a thorough rejection from every Division I program I solicited, I was forced to lower my college football expectations. My remaining options were to sign with a Division II team, go to a Junior College for two years, or walk on to a Division I program without a scholarship.

Coach Sochor showed a great deal of interest in me. He said I'd be a perfect fit for the student athlete philosophy at Davis. He told me that they had a Strong Safety named Andy San Juan who would be a senior the coming season, and who would probably go pro. Coach said I would have the chance to learn from Andy during my first year, and then start for the team for three years.

He had me at "pro".

Davis was building a reputation as one of the premier Division II football programs in the country. They were creating players who were making it to the National

Football League. And I would be learning directly
under their next pro player. It was a dream come true.

We had been in practices for about a week. Each day
consisted of two full practices and classroom sessions
learning the playbook, eating and sleeping. It was all
football, all the time. I loved it. I felt good. I was doing
well. Even better, we'd be starting full contact
practices soon, and it was then that I knew I would
shine. The plan Coach Sochor and I had made that
night at our dinner table was going to become reality.

Then IT happened.

The head defensive coach called me to his office. He
told me I was doing well. He said I would have a good
career at Davis and would be a valuable part of the
program. BUT... they had seen enough of me this year.
I was cut from the varsity and would be playing on the
freshman team.

WHAT?!

I was stunned. I walked out of his office feeling like
the little boy with tears in his eyes telling his mom he
was on the C team. But I wasn't a boy any more. I was
a man and I was determined to act like one.

I marched right into Coach Sochor's office. I
determinedly asked him if we could talk. I reminded
him of "our plan". I made my case. "How can you cut

me before we even started hitting?" I asked him. "I am a football player. I am a hitter, for goodness sake; I shine in the full contact of the real game, not doing exercises and drills."

He was persuaded. I practiced for two more weeks with the varsity team. But then the axe did fall. I was cut again, to the freshman team, where I remained for the year. While I was very disappointed, I soon discovered there were many other talented players on our freshman team. It wasn't as I wanted it to be but at least I was playing football.

MAN MEETS BENCH

After being cut from the varsity team as a freshman, I was determined to do better. I stayed in Davis the entire summer before my sophomore year focused on one thing; training for football. I had trained harder than ever before. This would be my break out year. I couldn't wait to get started. For the first time in my life I felt big, strong and fast.

I showed up for the first day of my sophomore year a full-sized man, 6' 2", 190 pounds, ready to play. Ready to hit. It was Wednesday night before our first game against Division IA Nevada Reno. Wednesday nights under the lights was a full contact, offense versus defense, battle of pride. It was also when the final starting line-ups where announced. We had a new defensive back (DB) coach that year. I had made a great impression on him all through the hot summer of double day practices. We had also developed a good rapport and he talked with me a lot.

Heading into our first game, I felt I was far and away the best Strong Safety. My DB coach had told me I was going to be starting. But that Wednesday evening, when the starting line-up was called, I heard this... "At Strong Safety... Dave Halliday." When I confronted my coach afterward, he assured me I'd be starting the following week. Next Wednesday evening... "Strong Safety... Dave Halliday." The pattern continued for a few more weeks. It was very strange. Although I didn't start, I played most of the time at away games, but hardly played at all during home games.

It was becoming the most frustrating year of my career. I had waited five long years to grow into my body. I had trained like a mad man. I had expected this to be my year and yet I hadn't started a single game. I finally resigned myself to the fact that there was something more than football going on. I committed to simply focusing on what I could control, and not worrying about anything else. At one point, around mid-season, I decided to relax, and have fun. And I'd never played better.

LEGACY OF BELIEF

My four years at U.C. Davis were a roller coaster ride. I have just shared a few of the lows with you. One of the highs was turning around a one-win, four-loss season in the middle of my junior year, to win seventeen straight games leading to the Division II National Championship my senior year. What a ride that was!

The biggest and most important high was being a part of what I call a legacy of belief. Jim Sochor's coaching philosophy was deeply influenced by the spiritual teachings of the Tao Te Ching. Coach believed that when you go with life and its natural laws, life is really not that hard and you'll have a great chance to succeed.

When coaching, he didn't use fancy words or esoteric eastern philosophy with us. Instead he translated the lessons taught by the Tao into language we would understand. When I interviewed Coach Sochor[20] years later, he said, "The most important thing I taught the team was to be self-referral."

Self-referral meant we were expected to take personal responsibility for how we prepared. Coach Sochor taught his staff and players that success is not about luck, or breaks, or injuries, or where you play. Even the opponent became relatively insignificant. If a starter was injured, his replacement was expected to be ready, fully prepared, and able to perform all aspects of the game plan. No excuses.

He taught us that our power comes from within. Coach Sochor and the culture he created within our football team re-enforced my parents' teaching that I could accomplish anything I set my mind to if I was willing to work long enough and hard enough for it.

When I think back to "our plan" at the dinner table with Coach Sochor, and talking about replacing Andy San Juan, and then starting for three years, nothing, I mean nothing, went according to plan, except one thing. The U.C. Davis, Division II Football Program had prepared me to go pro.

THREE STRIKES, YOU'RE OUT

One month after my final college football season ended I married my college sweetheart. One month after that, I signed a contract with the Saskatchewan Roughriders. I didn't know anything about Canadian football but was told my position, Strong Safety, didn't actually exist there. "Not to worry," they said, I would be playing a Linebacker position that was "similar to mine". But they wanted me to gain twenty-five pounds in two months, and report to camp at 210 pounds.

The two months of training that followed were awful. In addition to football drills, weight lifting, and running, I was eating like a crazy man. I would stuff myself full of a meal, and then go running. I had to put on weight faster than I thought was possible, and get in the best shape of my life, at the same time.

Arriving in Saskatoon, it soon became clear that I had packed more stuff than any other player. I moved into my training camp dormitory with a trunk full of my possessions. I was planning to stay the season.

The first sign of trouble was the moment I lined up in my new position. I was three yards off the line of scrimmage, starring right into the eyes of the right-side offensive Guard. This wasn't "like" Strong Safety at all. I was trying out for Middle Linebacker for a professional football team.'

By the end of the first week in camp, I can remember starting to "get a feel" for my new position. No sooner had I begun thinking it may be possible to make it than I was called into my coach's office and cut from the team.

Upon returning home, I went immediately back to training. I was determined to play professional football and one messed-up attempt, in the wrong position, in Canada, was not going to stop me. When I wasn't training, I did all the other things required in my life: going back to college to complete my economics degree, working part time as a bartender and in a hardware store, and coaching a high school football team.

Finally, I got another break. I had my workout with Axel Schmidt and was signed by the Raiders. I made it through all the mini camps and through the main training camp in Santa Rosa at the El Rancho Tropicana. I was cut on the Thursday before the first preseason game against my hometown San Francisco 49ers.

Three months later, I sat in my little apartment, on Drake Boulevard, in Concord, California reading through a United States Football League Player Contract, from the Orlando Renegades. It was the third such contract I was offered in less than two years. Only this time, it was different. In just four months, one of the most important events of my life was going to happen. My wife was five months pregnant. I was going to be a father for the first time. It was crystal clear what I must do. I was a football player. I signed the contract. I trained with every bit of focus and energy I could muster. I left in January and would return after the season to pick up the pieces of the lives I'd leave behind.

As it turned out, I was cut from the Renegades after just a few days. Our daughter Kaileen Elise was born on March 29, 1985, and I was there with her after all.

So, despite all the ups and down, and albeit for a short time, I had completed my transformation into a professional football player. This is a good moment to look at the three questions and my answers to them during my football years.

WHAT?: Become a pro football player.

WHY?: I had an inner drive to become the very best I could be.

HOW?: Singular focus. Hard work. A never, ever quit /never give up attitude.

Result: Three relatively short stints on pro teams, which all ended in me being cut... and many invaluable life lessons.

Who I became: A hard-hitting psycho who wanted to conquer the limitations of my body. I transformed from a normal school boy into a single-minded, selfish athlete with intense focus on and specialization in one thing. I was willing to do almost anything to become a professional football player, even to miss the birth of my first child. Football was everything to me.

MBG Life Lesson: I can accomplish anything I set my mind to if I am willing to work long enough and hard enough for it.

MBG Life Lesson: I'd rather follow my own dreams and fail than conform to "what I am supposed to do" and succeed.

GRATITUDE

I'd like to add a bonus section to this chapter explaining a lesson of gratitude I learned as a result of my football transformation.

During the summer of 1984, as I was training for the Raiders, I received a piece of advice that transformed my life. I had just been cut from the Rough Riders and I wanted desperately to play professional football. I was seeking advice. I was looking for magic. I wanted someone to just tell me what to do to succeed.

One of my lifelong friends, Mike Finn, was playing for the St. Mary's College football team in Moraga, California. His position coach Randy McClure was a former professional player for the Houston Oilers. I asked Mike if he would make an introduction. His coach was gracious and agreed to meet me. During our conversation, I asked him about his career, and how he made the leap from college to the pros. I asked him what advice he could share that could make a difference for me. Of course, there was no magic he could offer. He told me to keep doing what I was doing. He reminded me that at each step of the game, through four years of high school and four years of college, I had done what was needed to succeed. He told me to keep working hard, to trust in my abilities, and to be myself. As we parted, he shared a quote that has profoundly impacted my life...

"Your day belongs to another's dream." (The author is unknown to me)

Coach McClure was trying to shift my perspective — from chasing more and wanting life to be different, to being grateful and accepting my life as it was. He wanted me to understand that no matter what happened with the Raiders, I was already successful in football. It was his way of showing me that many other football players dreamed of being in the situation I was in... earning an opportunity to become a pro. He wanted me to acknowledge and appreciate what I had already accomplished.

The quote influenced me in ways that went far beyond football. It has been my reminder every day since that there are people in this world who can only dream of my daily experience as an American man, living in a country with the freedom to create the life I desire, and the opportunity to pursue my dreams. It is my constant reminder to be grateful for whatever I have in the moment. The quote helps me maintain perspective about the ups and the downs of life with humility. This was a big and important lesson for me.

My definition of perspective is getting beyond the personalization of success and failure. It means realizing that "I" am only one variable of many that may be responsible when life is in a "down" cycle. It also means not grabbing credit when life is on the "up" swing. Again, "I" am only one piece of the larger puzzle creating the current state of my life. This quote helps me shift my focus off of my ego (my head) and put it where it belongs (my heart), focusing me on being grateful for what I have in the moment. It helped me view my entire ten year football career as a great success because of what I accomplished rather than as a failure because it ended short of my ultimate goal. It was a powerful lesson I learned as a young man that has served me well in all the transformations that followed.

> *MBG Life Lesson*: Your day belongs to another's dream.

Chapter 7 - The Provider
(1985 – 2007)

"My children taught me the true meaning of
unconditional love."
(Yvonne Pierre)

Alone, at night, in the second bedroom we had
converted into a nursery, sitting in a brand new
rocking chair, I reflected on the day's events.

I was a father. Wow! Amazing!!

Just hours earlier, I held my beautiful, little daughter
in my arms. I experienced feelings of pure love and
beauty that I'd never felt before. The nurse told me
Kaileen was trying to suckle, and it would comfort her
if I let her suck on a finger while I held her.

The last two months had been very difficult for me. As
I wrote in the previous chapter, there was some
screw-up with the Renegades. They had me playing
Cornerback rather than Strong Safety, and cut me in
just two days – that was it... I had been cut from every
professional football league that existed at the time. I
had no more prospects. Football was over! Now what
was I going to do?

Upon returning home the day they gave me the news, I was angry, relieved, confused, and embarrassed. I was an emotional wreck. It was the first and only time in my life I think I felt what depression must be like. I had no direction. I had no money. I had no career prospects (nor even career ideas). I felt completely lost.

Slowly, I began reassembling the life I had left to become a pro football player. I went back to work at the hardware store and bar, and re-enrolled in college. I was going through the motions but I didn't know where I was going. For the last ten years, I had been working towards a goal. I had had clarity of purpose, every day. Now, I realized I needed to move on but I didn't know to *what*, and I had even less idea about *why*. Forget *how*. I didn't have any feeling deep in my heart about what I was to do next.

Until I held Kaileen in my arms, that was. Then I knew.

Sitting there, quietly, surrounded by the bright, primary colors, and the happy clown theme of her nursery, I knew.

Sitting there, sucking my index finger to see if I could suck as powerfully as my brand new, little baby, I knew.

Lightning Bolt: That night, I knew deep down inside me that it was time for me to grow up, get on with my life, and provide for my family. I had a new clarity of purpose. It was my responsibility to give Kaileen everything she needed to become happy and successful in life. What an enormous duty. What an amazing gift!

CHOOSING BUSINESS

As it turned out, my fifth-grade self had been right to say, *"If I don't get on a football team, I'll have a lot of thinking to do."*

I certainly did. Outwardly, it appeared that I needed to transform my entire way of thinking. During my football life, I'd made decisions based on how something affected my ability to become a better player. If it supported my goal to improve as a player, I did it. Everything else was secondary.

To become a provider, I needed to consider how my decisions affected my ability to provide for my family. I had to think about how my life impacted on others. I needed to learn to think of others first, and myself second. To be successful in my role as a provider, I had to shift from a selfish perspective to a more selfless focus on others.

With a new purpose, my old process worked just fine. I would now make decisions based on how something affected my ability to provide for my family. If it supported my goal to be a good provider, I would do it. Everything else would be secondary.

The first casualty of my new outlook was my desire for a career as an educator. I wanted to continue coaching. However, I decided a career in business would help me become a better provider. I was willing to do almost anything if it helped me provide for my family. I would work hard, learn fast, and pay attention. I would follow opportunity wherever it took me. Choosing business set me on a twenty-three-year journey that would include working in six different jobs, living in five houses, in four states, with three big cross-country moves, raising two children. And it would end in one very bitter divorce.

DRUG DEALERS

I graduated from college, went to work full time at the hardware store, and moved my young family out of our tiny apartment into a rental home with three bedrooms and lots of space. It was just on the other side of town, in a lower income neighborhood. About a year after living there, we returned home from an outing and I noticed the front door had been jimmied open. We cautiously entered our house to see what had happened. The TV and stereo were there, but our bedroom had been ransacked. The thieves had taken some of my wife's jewelry. The police told me what I already knew: Our next-door neighbors were drug dealers, and, while there was no evidence, they were the prime suspects. I decided there and then that I had allowed my family to live in this dangerous environment too long.

We began to look around and found ourselves a beautiful little house, in a brand new development in Pittsburg, California. Growing up in the pleasant surroundings of Walnut Creek, I was wary of crime "out there" in Pittsburg. But as a young family, just getting started, it was the place we could afford. It was clean, new, and only a short walk to the elementary school.

I was determined to move my family out of the danger of our rental house in Concord and buy the new house in Pittsburg. We could definitely afford the monthly mortgage with the recent pay increase I'd been given at the hardware store, but we had no money for the down payment. I asked every family member and friend I could think of, but I was unable to borrow what I needed.

So, I decided to take my case to the top. Football had taught me how to respectfully but forcefully state my case to the authorities in my life. For example, confronting Coach Sochor at U.C. Davis helped me earn two more weeks with the varsity team, and helped me stand out amongst other freshmen in the eyes of our coaching staff. When the Orlando Renegades cut me as a Cornerback, I marched directly into my coach's office to make sure he knew they had made a mistake. In that instance, all I got was the satisfaction of being heard. However, my football experiences taught me a valuable lesson that I would use my entire life:

> *MBG Life Lesson*: When I have a problem, I take it to the top.

So, I went to the wealthiest man I knew. Marc Kaplan was the son of the owner of the hardware store where I was employed, and the company's President. I had just finished my degree at U.C. Davis, in Economics. I had recently been promoted from a sales person on the retail floor to a Buyer in the company's main offices. It was a full-time, professional job. It came with a nice increase in pay.

I didn't really know Marc. He was the top executive and I was a lowly new hire in the back offices. But this was important. I needed to get my family out of harm's way. I had to muster the courage to ask for his help. So I made an appointment to see him.

I told Marc about the robbery. I made sure he knew I was the provider for my wife and baby daughter. I described the house I wanted to buy, and reviewed the details of our household budget to show we could afford it, with plenty left over to repay a loan. Then I asked him if I could borrow five thousand dollars. He told me he'd heard good things about me and said I would have an opportunity to build a career with his company. And he said he'd have the down payment money for me the following day. On a handshake, my relationship with the top man changed forever, my confidence to take problems to the top was re-enforced, and my financial ability to buy a home for my family was secured.

TEACHERS APPEAR

Six months into my job as a Buyer at the hardware store, a buzz at the door alerted the warehouse manager. He rolled open the large receiving door to find a truckload full of hardware. The problem was that his receiving floor was packed full and he was not expecting another delivery that day. He immediately called Art Simon to find out what was going on. Art was in charge of the merchandising department and was the company's Vice-President. He was also my boss. The problem is Art didn't know about this delivery either. So Art called the Hardware Buyer into his office. He intended to get to the bottom of it. And, at the bottom of it, he found *me*.

I had been learning so many things as a new Buyer. It felt like a true calling to me. I was learning to develop and manage business plans, research and select new product lines, negotiate supplier programs and terms, set pricing, and develop advertising campaigns. I was in charge of two profit centers; paint supplies and hardware.

I had just finalized my first big hardware deal. I had been impressed with a new supplier and so I'd given them the opportunity to make a big statement in our stores. In exchange, I received great payment terms and lots of advertising money. I was proud of what I'd achieved. This program would be great for the company, and excellent for my hardware profitability.

But Art wasn't so proud of me right at that moment. I got that feeling when he asked me to close the door as I entered his office. He then proceeded to give me a tough-love smack down.

> Art: "Did you schedule this delivery in advance with the warehouse?"

> Me: "Uhhm, no…"

> Art: "Have you prepared the hardware floor managers for this new program?"

> Me: "No."

> Art: "Have you notified Accounts Payable of what the program will cost and when the payment is due?"

> Me: "No."

Art: "Have you communicated with advertising about the promotional funds available?"

Me: "No."
Art: "Do you realize how much of a mess you create when you operate in a vacuum?"

Me: "I am beginning to, yes."

Art pointed out, in no uncertain terms, that I was a part of an intricate business system. Every time one part moves, it affects other parts. He called me irresponsible. He explained that I had better realize that with the authority to run my little businesses comes great responsibility, and I'd better realize it fast.

That day, feeling embarrassed and angry in his office, I wasn't able to see that a teacher had entered my life. But I soon came to understand how fortunate I was to have his guidance. Over the coming years, Art would mentor me on the art of business. He taught me all the basic functions of being a good Buyer, but he also invested his time and attention in teaching me about the importance of vision, teamwork, communication, and considering the impact of my decisions on others. Art wasn't just teaching me how to do my own job better, he was training me to become a business executive: To think like an owner.

THUMB SUCKER

The Pittsburg house was good for us. We grew our family there with the birth of our son Kyle in 1989. Kaileen attended the local elementary school from kindergarten through fourth grade and also started a swimming career that would one day earn her a college scholarship. Kyle had peaceful years as a toddler under the loving care of his mother and attended his first year of school there. I continued to learn and develop as a Buyer at the hardware store, and remained there for a total of eight years, until, in 1994, I was presented with an opportunity to switch from buyer to seller. I left the hardware store and joined a small manufacture representative firm where I worked and learned another aspect of retail business. Less than a year later, I was offered another job, as an auditor, and that changed everything. I jumped at it, and after five happy years in our Pittsburg house, we were on the move again.

It was the first day of our cross-country move from California to Kansas. I was driving my beautiful, black Infiniti Q45, and my wife was driving her white Jeep Grand Cherokee. She had Cody, our big black Doberman, with her. Ten-year old Kaileen was in Washington State, as she had qualified for a regional championship swim meet. After the meet, her chaperone would escort her to the airport and she would be flying to our new home. Kyle, now six, would alternate between riding with his mother and me.

This was a big move. I had grown up figuring I would always live in California, and now it was in my rearview mirror, rapidly disappearing. We were leaving our families behind. I was leaving the retail business and beginning anew, in an industry I knew nothing about. I was thinking about the magnitude of this transformation for all of us.

As I glanced at Kyle in the rearview, I felt so lucky to have him, and Kaileen – my two adorable, healthy, happy children.

Kyle was a beautiful boy. He had a natural affinity for numbers. And he loved balls. We would play catch and count the number of times we passed the ball without a drop. And for some reason, he loved the Miami Dolphins football team. He actually cried upon learning that Head Coach Don Shula had retired following the Dolphins 1995 season.

Kyle was peaceful, happy and healthy... and he loved sucking his thumb. He had used it to comfort himself to sleep every single night. "You know, Kyle, if you decide to stop sucking your thumb, no one in Kansas will ever know that you did," I said to him, as we drove along. I don't recall that he said anything back to me when I made my comment, but he never sucked his thumb again. That was his quiet way, and still is. He takes information in and processes it on his own time. All previous attempts by my wife and me to stop

82

the thumb sucking had failed. But that day, those twenty-one words did it.

Teachers appear in all shapes and sizes. That day, my son taught me an important lesson about leading change. The right timing is important. The environment must be prepared properly. Most importantly, though, you have to clearly anchor the benefits of changing to something important, and create the power needed to overcome the forces of Gravity maintaining the status quo. I had Kyle at, "no one in Kansas will ever know."

TREASURE FINDER

The buyer at O'Reilly Auto Parts had just negotiated a dollar off the regular price of their best-selling car wash. He would be featuring the item as a loss leader for the summer advertising campaign. The manufacturer said the one-dollar discount would apply to all truckload orders delivered from Monday, May 1, 1995 through Friday, May 26, 1995. My new job as an auditor was to make sure deals like this were always transacted in favor of my client. I was in my office, at the old down town airport in Kansas City, surrounded by banker's boxes chock-full of purchase orders, invoices, deal sheets, and other business documents we had gathered from O'Reilly Auto Parts, looking for any errors that may have occurred which caused O'Reilly to pay more to a supplier than they should have.

In the first few months at my new job, I had learned that, on average, our clients pay their bills with 99.9% accuracy. That seems pretty good, doesn't it? But a one-tenth of a one percent error (0.1%) on $1 billion in purchases was $1 million, for example. When we found that million dollars, our client kept 50% ($500,000), and sent the other 50% ($500,000) to our company's headquarters in Dallas, Texas. Headquarters kept half ($250,000) and sent the rest ($250,000) to the franchise that did the finding. I was working for two women who owned the Kansas City franchise.

So, in the paper avalanche in my office that day, I found two invoices that looked like winners from the car wash deal. One was ordered on April 27 and delivered on May 2. The purchase order and invoice reflected the regular price. According to the deal sheet, "all truckload orders delivered from Monday, May 1, 1995 through Friday, May 26, 1995" would get the promotional price. One truckload has twenty-six pallets of car wash. Each pallet holds 64 cases. Each case contains 9 gallons. That's 14,976 gallons of car wash at one dollar each. I had just found $14,976. Finding errors like this one feels like hitting the jackpot on a slot machine. And the jackpots just kept on coming.

Another order was dated Monday, May 29. It was another full truckload of car wash. The auditors who trained me had explained that a retailer often places a promotional order just before a deal (getting ready) or just after (replenishing inventory from the promotion). In both cases, the order was "caused" by the promotion, and therefore, we reasoned, it should receive the discount. The May 29th order fit the "Before/After" model. I just found another $14,976 which O'Reilly had overpaid, fifty percent of which they would now receive back. It was like handing them money they hadn't even known they had.

My third big find of the day was a duplicate payment. I found a $9,200 invoice with an odd-looking invoice number. Upon investigation, my client had paid the invoice using the order number instead of the invoice number. The supplier didn't notice the mistake and so they sent the invoice again. My client paid it again, this time using the invoice number. I had just found another $9,200 for O'Reilly… $39,152 for the day! "Finding" money like this was very exciting, but the grueling process of manually sifting through stacks and stacks of boxes full of paper was not. I felt there must be a better way.

The frustrating process of manual auditing through reams of paper was not the only aspect of the auditing business that weighed heavily on me. During my four years in that role in Kansas, I was paid a monthly draw from the regional manager who hired me. It was enough money to meet our basic needs and not much more. In the auditing business, it takes time to organize an audit, then find the errors, then write the claims. Then the client collects the money, and then we get paid. For the first three years, my draw exceeded my share of the money I "found" and I steadily accumulated debt. At one point, I was nearly $200,000 in debt just from my work. Needless to say, it was a very stressful financial time in my life.

However, there were upsides. In the years that followed, I was given the opportunity to be part of the team leading the automation revolution for our recovery auditing business. It was with this opportunity that I learned the power of computing and data mining that would become so instrumental in my future success. And it was the opportunity that would help me get out of debt, too.

SPORTS DAD

The hunt for treasure in recovery auditing has an insidious pull. A bit like gambling, it feels like you will find the next big win in the next box of paper. There is no end: You can always audit more! I struggled to keep myself from working long hours, and from having my mind on the job even when I was at home. Eventually I realized that my working life was having a negative impact on my home life. I had to consider what was most important to me, and I knew that I needed to create a better balance in my life.

Being a provider did require me to build a successful career and make a good living. But it had other facets too. I needed to be in the home with my family. And this need for a balance of time and focus wasn't just an issue at my auditing job. During my fast-paced years at the hardware store, I was literally working ten-hour days and seven days a week. At one point during my buying days, I realized I was being sucked into my career like I had been sucked into football, to the detriment of my family. I made the commitment then to take Sunday off every week, and dedicate that time to being fully at home, mentally and emotionally, as well as physically. Later, as an auditor, I found more balance by taking advantage of the fact that I could set my own hours and work at my own speed. For the first time in my working career, I had the opportunity to work a regular Monday through Friday, 9:00 to 5:00 schedule, so I took it. And that gave me the opportunity to spend more time with my children, and led to me becoming a sports dad.

I agree with the well-known quote, "Sports do not build character, they reveal it."

I was pleased that Kaileen and Kyle were both interested in and participated in sports. It gave me the chance to provide love and support for them in the context of an activity of their choosing. Kyle loved basketball. When we moved to Kansas, he started playing as a first grader. The local league needed coaches, so I enlisted. I told Kyle I would continue coaching his teams as long as my coaching could keep up with the talent of the kids.

I loved coaching. It was an early sign of what would become my mission here at Happy Living to improve the health and wellbeing of the world, one person at a time. Coaching sports offered me the opportunity to teach and provide leadership to youngsters. My primary message to my little basketball players was self-responsibility. Perhaps this was my way of starting the kids down the path of self-referral that Coach Sochor had taught to me. I told every player it was his responsibility to try his best whenever he was on the court. It was his responsibility to pay attention when he was on the bench. And it was his responsibility to make it to every practice and every game. If he couldn't make it, it was his job to call me and let me know, not his parents' responsibility.

These were boys aged five through eight. I had them each sign a pledge of responsibility and I explained "my rules" to every parent. It worked great. The boys took on the challenge and even the parents behaved themselves! We had great fun as the boys became true team players. I coached Kyle's teams for another three years before resigning. I'm proud to say that the players' talent was advancing so far and fast that my coaching skills were no longer making the grade.

DREAM KILLERS, AGAIN?

"You probably think it's pretty good to be the second best in the world," Jeff said, "but to me, it was a devastating failure." Jeff Rouse was an Olympic champion from the 1992 Summer Olympics in Barcelona, Spain. I had invited him to share his Olympic story with the members of Kaileen's swim team and their parents.

Jeff had won the gold medal swimming for the winning U.S. team in the men's 4×100-meter medley relay, and a silver medal for his second-place performance in the men's 100-meter backstroke. It was this second-place performance that he was telling us about. You see, Jeff was the world record-holder of the Men's 100-meter backstroke at the time. He had trained for four years to be the best in the world when it mattered most; at the Olympic finals, in Barcelona.

And he had fallen short.

Kaileen had become a nationally-ranked swimmer by the time she was ten years old. She swam on year-round, competitive teams from age seven, when we were still living in Concord, California until she earned a swimming scholarship to the University of Nevada, Las Vegas.

Year-round swimming is a grueling, time-sucking sport, for the athletes and their parents. Swim meets were typically two or three-day events, starting early in the morning and continuing until late in the afternoon, each day. Parents often spent twenty to thirty hours at a meet in order to watch their child compete for a few races lasting anywhere between thirty seconds to ten minutes. There was a lot of down time, and a lot of time for talking.

Early in Kaileen's swimming career, I began noticing a familiar attitude. Parent after parent would compare their child to the "fast ones". They would say, out loud, that their child could never be as good. They were projecting their own limitations onto their child. Why *would* they do this? I wondered. Why *did* so many do this?

It was the dream-killer phenomenon all over again. Only this time I was the parent, and I had to do something about it!

So, I asked for a meeting with Kaileen's head swim coach. I explained my football story, including the part about the dream-killers. I shared how inspired I had been by Fred Biletnikoff. I told the coach what I had been hearing from so many of the parents, who were unwittingly acting as dream-killers. If they acted this way on the pool deck, I wondered, what could be going on in their homes?

I could see how dedicated the swimmers were. It was obvious they had the heart. It was clear they were willing to work hard and transform their bodies into successful swimming machines. I wanted to help them with the mental side, with "belief", as Fred Biletnikoff had helped me.

It was very rewarding organizing "mental toughness" programs for two of Kaileen's swim teams. Our programs were called *Terrapin Toughness* in Concord, California and *The Blazer's Edge* in Kansas City. It was an opportunity to inspire the swimmers and educate their parents that "normal" kids can achieve extraordinary results when they combine heart, hard work, and belief.

Jeff Rouse's message to our young swimmers was all about overcoming mental setbacks. When he was out-touched by Mark Tewksbury by 6/100's of a second, and lost what he considered "his" event, his mental toughness went into a tailspin. He felt like a complete failure. He was convinced that he had not only let himself down, but also his family, his team, and his country! He was an emotional wreck.

The problem was, he had to swim again, and soon. The Men's 4×100-meter medley relay final was coming up. The United States had never lost this event in the history of the Olympic Games. In the ready room, his teammates were growing concerned. It was clear that Jeff was still in an emotional funk and in no state to swim well.

Jeff told us that Pablo Morales, who would swim the Butterfly leg of the relay, took it upon himself to sort the situation out. "He got in my face!" Jeff explained. "He told me to snap out of it. He said I was the fastest backstroker in the world and that I had better get out there and act like it!" Well, you can imagine how much his young audience loved hearing that!

Jeff went on to say that something just clicked at that moment. He swam the first hundred meters beating Tewksbury, breaking his own world record, and giving his teammates the lead. The team went on to win the gold medal, and tie the world record. His message to us that day was this; we have within us the power to control our mind, or to be controlled by it.

It was an inspiring lesson. He taught us that even world champions battle with negative thoughts. He showed us that both negative and positive "switches" could be turned on in our minds. Inspired by Jeff, I learned to be more aware of my own mental roadblocks and negative thinking. Now, when I see them coming, I look for the Pablo Morales-type energy inside me and switch that on, full beam.

BAD DAD

On the flip side of dream-killers are those parents that push their children too hard. I have to hold my hand up and confess that I was one of those parents with my first two children. I believe the dream-killers were operating, most often, out of genuine love for their children. They didn't want them to be hurt if they failed to reach their goals. And as the dream-killers couldn't see how their goals were possible, failure seemed like the only outcome.

As a hard-pusher, I too was operating out of love. But I too was projecting my own "stuff" onto my children. I projected onto Kaileen and Kyle the desires of my youth; I had a very strong, inner drive to be the best, and I was willing to do almost anything to get there. I spent so much time and energy trying to "help" Kaileen and Kyle believe they could be the best that I never bothered to pay attention to what they wanted most. I presumed to know what was in their hearts rather than asking them what they truly wanted. I put way too much pressure on my children.

As an adult, Kaileen has told me:

> It felt like you were pushing us to be the best, the toughest, to work the hardest, even more than the other kids, or what our coaches asked of us. And if our effort faltered, or if we didn't believe in ourselves, that was "unacceptable!" — a word that even as an adult, I only hear in my mind from your voice!!!

I am so very sorry my children had to be the teachers to help me learn this lesson. And I feel proud beyond measure that they had the courage to hold onto their own senses of what they wanted during this time, and privileged that they feel able to communicate their feelings about it with me now so openly.

BIG TIME FOR LIFE

Four years after I started working for them, the auditing company had an opening for a regional manager. It was a corporate job responsible for overseeing a number of regional franchises. It was a good opportunity, but I had my mind set on something else as I waited in the lobby wearing my best suit. It was my first big, formal interview process. I would rotate through three different rooms and be interviewed by the top leaders of the company. None of them knew I was applying for a job I didn't want.

Our company was entering a period of rapid innovation. A perfect storm of improved electronic data management technology, more computing power, and sophisticated auditing routines was pulling us from the dark ages of manual processes into a brand new world of automated auditing.

Under the guidance of my regional manager and mentor, Jim Meehan, I had been tasked with improving the consistency of audits within his region. In doing so, I discovered a big opportunity, not just for Jim's region but also for the entire company. I found that all of his auditing centers were in the transition from manual to automated processes for their audits. The problem was that everyone was "reinventing the wheel" on their own. As a result we had audit centers all across the region using different technologies, different approaches, and getting different results while trying to solve the same problems. No one was working together. There was no sharing of best practices. In fact, most were not even documenting the practices being used. It was chaos. We were certainly not operating like the intricate business system Art Simon had taught me about. Rather than when "every time one part moves, it affects other parts", in this company when one part moved, the other parts didn't know anything else was moving.

Art had taught me to think like an owner. He'd mentored me about the importance of vision, teamwork, and communication within a company. Now, all these years later, I would use my interview opportunity to make the case for my vision for the auditing company. I would recommend creating a new department of strategic auditing, and I would convince them that I was the man to lead it.

As you can imagine, they were taken aback when I told them I didn't want the regional manager job. To their credit, they listened to my proposal, and my unorthodox interview worked! Several months later, I was moving my family again. Our destination was Plano, Texas. I was the new Vice President of Strategic Auditing. I was working in a wonderful office in the Dallas World Headquarters, and doing work that I loved. My first year I made so much money with the combination of my current year salary as a Vice President and the residual income from my previous year's audit recoveries that I was able to pay off nearly all my auditing debt.

My wife and I were very excited to have a big, beautiful new home, too. I had a senior role and a salary to match. I also had proximity to all the company executives and was cultivating important relationships, including with the CEO. Most importantly, I was doing work I loved and that I believed would revolutionize our company. And I was only thirty-eight years old.

I felt like I had hit the Big Time. I had found a company where I could really make an impact. I truly felt that I had found a place where I would work the rest of my life.

A few years later, though, the shocking news came; our company was to be sold to our number one competitor. My entire life plan had gone in a flash... again!

INFILTRATING HQ

When the largest company in a small, niche industry like accounts payable recovery auditing buys its number one competitor, there is bound to be lots of duplication in corporate office functions. That usually means layoffs for the company being acquired. I felt compelled to do something to keep my team together and save our jobs.

Our strategic auditing team had grown into a small group of five or six people, and we had been doing really good work. We were beginning to make a difference in our company's entire approach to auditing. Rather than describing an audit routine in a written manual so an auditor would recognize the error when he or she saw it on an invoice, we were writing audit routines as computer programs, and using the computer to find every invoice with the error, every time. Rather than spending time sifting through invoices, we were spending time sifting through the minds of experienced auditors. We were discovering every different type of error found by any auditor, for any client, and adding computerized routines to our growing library of best practices.

Our computerized approach was much faster, less expensive, and far more accurate and consistent than the processes we were replacing. I knew the change we were capable of bringing to *our* company, but what about our acquirer? What were they doing? Were we more or less advanced than them? I had to do something to find out.

Under the protective cover of a favorite phrase, "It's better to ask for forgiveness than to ask for permission", I purchased a plane ticket to Atlanta, the home of the corporate headquarters of the acquiring company.

Our two companies were deeply involved in the due diligence process associated with a major acquisition of this type. Due Diligence is the examination of every important aspect of a company that is being acquired including personnel, customers, finances, assets, technologies, intellectual property, etc. It typically involves many interviews by the acquiring company of key personnel of the target company, i.e. us. So, as I was walking around their headquarters in Atlanta, introducing myself as the Vice President of Strategic Auditing, they must have thought I'd been invited.

I met several important contacts that day. I was invited into their offices to explain what strategic auditing meant from our company's point of view. I was able to show them the cutting-edge work we had been doing, including telling them about our best practices library and showing them a presentation our team had prepared which illustrated the benefits of our automated approach.

My impulsive infiltration paid off. On Christmas Eve, I got the call saying me and my entire team would be keeping our jobs. Unfortunately, this great news wasn't the beginning of a wonderful new chapter for my team, though. For the two frustrating years that followed, I would spend most of my time trying to put a square peg in a round hole.

CHOOSING MOUNTAINS

In less than a week, I had fallen in love. For the first time in my life, I had spent an entire week skiing, and I had been bitten by the bug. In the final few days, I was gliding down the beautiful, snowy mountainside of the Winter Park Resort with relative ease. I wasn't alone. Kyle, who was in the eighth-grade then, had spent the week snowboarding. He was in love too.

Heading back to the airport, we stopped in a wonderful little town called Evergreen. We "just looked" at a few homes. Throughout our vacation, we had imagined what it would be like to move to the mountains. We'd had conversations like that on our trips before, as everyone does, but this time it felt different.

> *Lightning Bolt:* Back at work, and back at home on the flat plains of North Texas, I couldn't get the mountain lifestyle out of my mind.

I started thinking about the pros and cons of a possible move to the mountains.

On the 'pro' side:

- Kaileen was in her last year of high school and would be leaving to attend, and swim for, the University of Nevada, Las Vegas in August.

- Kyle was in his last year of middle school. He would be starting at a new high school anyway, whether here or there.

- My wife was unhappy in Plano, and our marriage was beginning to unravel. Perhaps a move would be refreshing for us both, and for our relationship.

- My wife had family living in Winter Park. It was their home that we had stayed in during our vacation.

On the 'con' side:

- We had moved Kyle nearly every four years since he was born, and our priority now was to give him some control over his life. If he wanted to stay in Plano with his friends, that would trump everything and we would have to wait four years until he completed high school and went to college, and then move.

Clearly the pro side was the winner but the con side had ultimate veto power. Kyle was excited by the idea of moving, but was torn about leaving the friends he had made. In the end my clever son's savvy side came out and I had to sweeten the deal to secure his approval. With the promise of season tickets at Winter Park every year, we brought Kyle on board.

We were all excited. We were headed to the beautiful mountains of Colorado.

We returned to Evergreen that spring and bought a home, and later that same summer, we moved in. This was to be my first of three moves across the country driven by lifestyle. Colorado was great for me. I loved just about everything about it. We lived in a beautiful home on a mountainside. We had a great view from the back of the house, and a hot tub in the back yard with the best view of all.

Nature had a wonderful way of seeping into my life there. We had evergreen trees and mountains as far as the eye could see. Animal life was ever-present. We couldn't leave a trashcan on the curb at night because bears would come. Deer were regularly seen from our patio. A drive through town could be interrupted by a parade of elk.

I often exercised in the wilderness. Within ten minutes, I could be deep in solitude on one of many beautiful hiking trails in the area. I spent many hours "out there", exercising, thinking, reflecting, and relaxing my mind. In the winter, we skied. It took just over an hour from driveway to ski run. We made that drive often. Every summer, Kyle and I enjoyed a weeklong, boys-only rafting trip exploring one gorgeous river or another. Even during the short drive to the gym, the beauty of the place surrounded me.

Perhaps my favorite part of Colorado was my hot tub. I would end most every day there, and Kyle would frequently join me. If I was alone, it was a great time to relax and take in the magnificence of the mountain. I had many break-through thoughts and ideas sitting there. One evening, a poem just came to me, in a matter of minutes. It was about the older brother I never knew. Very sadly, he died shortly after his birth. I was the replacement child.

My Angel at Heaven's Gate

You were me, until I became you
It was God's wish... there was nothing we could do

The Master's plan required that you would go to Him
Then He put me here on earth in the space you would have been

The space He let me fill has been like a heaven on earth
My life has been so blessed... full of love, happiness and mirth

It was many years until I understood my fate
I was born with my own special angel living at Heaven's gate

I can now reflect back on my wonderful life
and see the many moments your grace helped
me through strife

I have walked with a calm and confidence that
often unnerved another
If they only knew my secret, I was given
strength from my brother

I am so grateful for the gift given to me at my
birth
I await our wondrous meeting when my time
ends here on earth

I jumped out of the hot tub and wrote it down as soon
as I could so I wouldn't lose any of the words.

When Kyle was with me in the hot tub, we talked. I
talked with Kyle during our first four years in Colorado
more than all of his other years combined, before and
after. We found special time to be together on our
drives to ski the mountain too, and also on our rafting
trips. We talked about everything, from the silly to the
serious. The breadth of knowledge Kyle possessed at a
young age amazed me. Our times together in
Colorado really deepened our relationship, and I feel
honored to have had them.

YOU'RE FIRED, TWICE

There was a nearly-daily clash of cultures going on at new company after the acquisition. Two years later, as I was sitting in a conference room on the executive floor of our company's headquarters in Atlanta, one of my colleagues called me an iconoclast. I had to ask what it meant. He said an iconoclast is a person who attacks cherished beliefs or institutions. He was right - that's exactly what the report I was preparing for the CEO would do. Ever since the acquisition, there has been friction between the fundamental strategies of the two companies.

My old company, and I, believed that the lead auditor, as the person with the closest relationship to and knowledge of the client, should be the final decision-maker for all auditing matters. We believed it was headquarters' role to develop technologies, processes and services that would enable leaders in the field to conduct their audits better, faster, and more cost-effectively. It was our view that headquarters existed to serve the field.

My new company believed exactly the opposite. They were developing technologies, processes, and services to pull more and more decision-making into centralized control. They believed centralization was the key to conduct faster, more accurate, and more profitable audits. It was their view that staff in the field existed to serve headquarters.

I had been tasked with a top-level assignment to visit audit centers across the country, from both companies (old and new), and make a recommendation for a go-forward strategy directly to the CEO. During my audit site visits, I uncovered a consistent and disturbing fact; our customers were growing tired of paying us to correct invoices with the same mistakes year after year. They wanted us to help them correct their systems so they wouldn't make the mistakes in the first place.

I recommended that we should expand on my old company's model of empowering our field auditors. We should shift the strategy to empower our customers. We could re-purpose our audit knowledge, technologies, processes, and services to enable our clients to fix their corporate systems and processes, and prevent errors from happening in real time, rather than having to correct them years later.

This strategy would have revolutionized the company and the industry. It would have changed us from a service provider to a software provider. It would have transformed our field workers from auditors to audit coaches. We could have significantly reduced the numbers of employees needed in the company, dramatically increased profitability and, most importantly, given our clients what they wanted and needed.

It was during my impassioned sharing of this new strategy with my colleagues that one called me an iconoclast. All the others agreed with him. They warned me I had not properly understood my assignment. They said I was tasked with visiting audit centers across the country to create a report that told the CEO what he wanted to hear. I was supposed to confirm that centralization was the way of the future. Then I could help convince the leaders from my old company to get on board, or get off the train.

If I took *my* report to the CEO, my colleagues warned me, I would be fired.

I did it anyway.

And they were right.

Seven months after moving to Colorado, I was suddenly without a job.

The next three and a half years were a whirlwind of challenge. I started two different businesses and bought another. Each business lost money, each year… totaling more than $750,000 at one point. At the end of year three, a major business loan had gone into default. And then my wife of nearly twenty-four years fired me too.

Being in Colorado hadn't helped my marriage as I had hoped. With each passing year, more and more of the stitching holding my wife and me together unraveled. She didn't seem to be any happier in the mountains than she'd been on the Texas plains. Or perhaps she was just growing unhappy with me, or with herself. I don't feel it's my place to speculate, but what I do know is this; our relationship grew more and more contentious.

I remained committed to our wedding vows and figured I was just getting a super heavy dose of the "bad times". I protected myself and my sanity by spending more and more time outside the house... hiking, skiing, rafting, hot-tubbing, and lots and lots of business travel.

Kyle had graduated from high school and had moved out of the house to begin his first year at the University of Colorado in Boulder. I held a glimmer of hope that "empty-nesting" could slowly revive our marriage, but things only got worse. On September 18, 2007, we had our last huge fight. It was bad. I was bleeding and I had to get out. Driving down the long winding road at midnight, I was pulled over by police coming up the other way. My wife had called the cops, on me, making accusations. It was one of the lowest points of my life. There I was, locked in the back seat of a patrol car, in my own driveway, in the middle of the night. I knew the truth, and I had told the police what really happened. But it seemed like they were in there forever. When they finally emerged through the front door, my wife was in their custody.

I was released.

That night turned out to be the culmination of a series of events that ended my first marriage. The fighting was finally over.

I spent the following week alone in my house, in deep contemplation. I tried endlessly to determine what I was meant to learn from this horrible event. My emotions moved from shock and sadness to hope and freedom. As I realized that my life had changed suddenly and permanently, two thoughts began circling through my mind:

1. A thought about the book *Good to Great*.

2. A thought about paying attention to what you're attracted to, deciding what you want, and then acting on it.

Good to Great[21], by Jim Collins, is one of my favorite business books. It is about companies that were *good* for many years and suddenly became *great*. The author and his team of researchers quantified great companies by how much they outperformed their competition. The book revealed an inflection point when each company transformed from good to great. Then it compared what the great companies did differently from the good companies.

I was a healthy, forty-six-year-old father of two grown children, with a new business. It's true that it was losing money but it was full of potential. As I reflected on my life up to that point, I concluded that it had indeed been a good one. But this moment was an inflection point for me. I was determined to figure out what I could do to create a great life from there on out.

The Secret[22], by Rhonda Byrne, was the inspiration for my other circling thought. I was in a unique position to re-craft my life. My long, difficult marriage was over. I had raised my children into adulthood. In the domestic sense, I was free. And, although I'd always be pleased to help and support my children if asked, of course, I had completed my goal of being the provider for my family. I could do and be whatever I wanted.

So, my first task was to decide exactly *what* that was.

It was time for me to pay attention to what I was attracted to. I would make a fresh start and create a great life. I started paying close attention to what inspired me. The things that most attracted me in life were signals or messages telling me what I truly wanted, somewhere deep inside me. Those signals would lead me on a new path for my life.

On September 27, 2007, I moved out of the big house, into a dumpy little condo, and began my transformation from good to great.

Staying active outside the house had saved me during the final four years of my marriage, but it hadn't saved Kyle. I didn't realize the heavy toll those years took on him. It was only after the marriage had ended that Kyle confided, and I actually listened, about how hard it had been for him "in the house" with his mother when I was away. In my dumpy condo, without my beloved hot tub or mountaintop views, my children and I shared our best holiday together in many, many years.

BAD DAD, AGAIN

I'd been trying to do the right thing by standing by my vows, and hoping that things would work out if I gave them more time, but Kaileen and Kyle both told me that it would have been way better for them had the marriage ended earlier. I deeply regret the pain which that time caused my children. I wish I had had the strength, or courage, or wisdom, or whatever it was that I didn't have, to spare them the damage caused by my failing relationship with their mother.

Here are the three questions and my answers to them during my provider years.

WHAT?: To be the provider for my family.

WHY?: Responsibility, duty, love.

HOW?: I choose the 'provider' path of business rather than the comfortable path of teacher and coach. I paid attention, followed opportunity wherever it took me, worked hard and learned fast. I made decisions based on providing love, support, and leadership for my family.

Result: I raised two beautiful children and provided opportunities for them to succeed. I gained twenty-four years' worth of experience learning about life, love, and relationships.

Who I became: A kinder, gentler and more balanced man. Choosing the role of provider helped me become a better father to my children. Choosing the path of business prepared me for the next big transition of my life.

These are the other life lessons which came out of that time:

MBG Life Lesson: When you want to lead change, clearly demonstrate the benefits of changing to others.

MBG Life Lesson: We have within us the power to control our minds or to be controlled by them.

MBG Life Lesson: My dreams are mine alone. I cannot presume that others think like me or want what I want.

MBG Life Lesson: Be bold and ask for what you want. Boldness has genius, power, and magic in it.

MBG Life Lesson: Take the risk, act when you're scared, it's unlikely that you'll be eaten today.

MBG Life Lesson: It's hard to distinguish between good luck and bad luck[23]. Many of the highest points in my life have led to low points, and visa versa.

MBG Life Lesson: It's better to ask for forgiveness than to ask for permission.

Chapter 8 - Business Man
(2003 – 2014)
"No institution in America is freer to do what it wants
to do than a business."
(Unknown)

My transformation from a provider working for someone else to a business man working for myself began the moment I was fired from the auditing company in 2004. But the truth is, I had dreamed of becoming a business owner most of my adult life.

I made a decision in 2003 that I would start my own company that I could build slowly while still working as an employee. I had settled on the business of "flipping houses" (buying a house in need of repair, making all the necessary improvements, selling it, and then reinvesting the profits into the next house). I had read a few books, created a financial plan, and filed all the paperwork to become a limited liability company (LLC). I intended to buy my first "fixer-upper" in 2004. Before that could happen, though, I received the fateful news that the auditing company was terminating my employment.

I was fired on a Thursday. I was now free to put my ideas about the future of auditing into practice and that was way more exciting than flipping houses. The very next day I went to work changing my LLC from a

113

home remodeling business to an audit recovery business. For nearly six months I worked on developing the business plan, creating marketing materials and prospect lists, and making sales calls. Then another opportunity looked so great I completely switched gears again. This time, I changed my LLC from the audit recovery business to an investment company. By the end of 2004, my LLC had invested in two companies that provided services to large, multi-national businesses. These two companies helped their customers manage custom requirements when shipping products across international borders. These were the two companies I mentioned in the last chapter that had lost more than $750,000 in my first three years of ownership.

The seven years between 2007 and 2014 were very busy, including another cross country move, a steamy love affair, a marriage, adoptions, and a complete turn-around of my two companies. I'll be sharing the stories of these life-changing events in later chapters. For now, I'd like to jump to the end of the business story and then carefully reveal the steps involved in turning the companies around, merging the two into one customs company, and ultimately selling it in 2014 for $42,100,000.

So, let's zoom forwards to 2014...

I was alone, driving on Highway 40 on the first of four days of a road trip across the country. It was Friday,

May 30. My new family and I were moving from Camp Verde, Arizona to Mooresville, North Carolina. My wife, Dani, whom I had married nearly five years earlier, and our two daughters, Shea and Sydney, whom I had adopted shortly after our marriage, had left by plane the day before.

I pulled over at a roadside rest area for lunch. I had packed lunchmeats, cheese and pickles in an ice chest, and had plenty of bottled water. Sitting behind the car, in my folding camping chair, with the tailgate open, it was perhaps the most memorable lunch of my entire life.

So much had happened since I began my transformation from good to great back in 2007.

Now, I could finally celebrate. Thirty minutes earlier, I had received a text message with the news I was waiting for. The deal had officially closed, and millions of dollars had been wired to my personal bank account.

The previous week had been a whirlwind caused by horrible timing. We had bought our home in North Carolina in September, closed on it in December, and then scheduled our move for the last week of May, after school was over for the girls.

We decided to sell the customs company in January with the closing scheduled for the end of March or first of April at the latest. The due diligence process of selling our company was the single greatest organizational challenge of my life. Seemingly everything that could go that could go wrong did go wrong. Much to my dismay, the three days the movers were in our house packing everything, including my home office, was also the final three days of our closing period. Both the move and the closing would have been enough by themselves to keep me extremely busy, but when they happened at the same time it created a comedic scene that I was barely able to keep up with.

Our home had two levels; the main floor and a walk out basement. The movers were unable to get their large truck down the driveway, so, at one point, I was driving my pick-up truck across our rock yard to the lower level. The movers would load up the truck bed and I'd drive back across the yard, up our long driveway, to the moving truck. I did this for hours on the final day. At the same time, I was responding to emails, and participating in conference calls. I was furiously hammering out the final negotiations and agreeing to the documentation for selling the company... from my pick-up truck.

When I wasn't "operating" out of my truck, I was doing business from a mobile internet hub my wife had set up for me, as the service to the house had been turned off. My mobile office for the three moving days was a foldable camping chair, and my

116

brief case and laptop computer. I constantly moved from room to room to find a quiet work place, based on the progress of the moving crew.

The movers were supposed to begin on Tuesday and be finished on Wednesday. I was planning to drive my wife and daughters down to Phoenix on Thursday, have a celebratory dinner at my brother-in-law's home, take them to the airport Friday morning, and then begin my four-day drive to North Carolina.

Instead, the movers didn't finish until after 9:00 PM on Thursday. I had to remain there to supervise the move and lock up the house. My parents volunteered to take my family to Phoenix and let me stay at their home in Prescott Valley that night.

It wasn't what I'd planned, but at least the chaos of the move was finally over.

I drove the forty-five minutes to my parent's home where we had a wonderful but brief celebration. I signed the final closing document the following morning, on their dining room table.

The chaos of selling the company was finally over, too.

UNEXPECTED KINDNESS

After all the upheaval and emotion that comes with such huge life changes, I was very excited to have four days to be alone. It gave me time to reflect on the nearly ten years of growing the business, and the solitude I needed to quiet my mind, and think deeply about what I wanted to do in the next phase of my life.

The first day's drive ended in Albuquerque, New Mexico. My wife had called to say that she and the girls had arrived safely in North Carolina. All was good.

After checking in to my hotel, I walked around downtown Albuquerque in search of dinner. Upon finding the perfect restaurant, I settled into my table, ordered dinner, and started reading my book. After a while, I noticed a small group at the table next to me. They were having a great time and laughing a lot. The gentleman started some small talk with me, sharing that it was his wife's birthday. They were clearly very nice people and a fun family.

I was feeling very happy and wanted to do something special. I asked my waiter to put the birthday party's tab on my bill. As you can imagine, they were very surprised about and appreciative of my unexpected kindness. The group introduced themselves and invited me for an after-dinner drink. I thanked them but declined. I was ready to turn in for the night and reflect on the day's events.

We said goodnight and parted ways.

When I arrived back to my hotel, I noticed the birthday party at the front desk. They had followed me to my hotel and again asked if they could buy me a drink. I had to accept this time. We sat at the rooftop bar and got to know each other. It was a lovely evening. It felt like I had met six new friends. I went to bed feeling very happy, very grateful, and very tired. I woke the next morning, packed my stuff, and walked down to the lobby to check out. To my surprise, the group had paid for my hotel stay and left a handwritten card of thanks.

Wow!

This is how it happens. One unexpected act of kindness leads to another, and then another, and so on. Acts of kindness create more kindness. From that day forward, I have been determined to look for opportunities to practice random acts of kindness.

GLORY DAYS

As my cross-country journey continued, I began to grasp the magnitude of this moment in my life. The last ninety days had been a blur. I sold a company I'd spent the past ten years building. I'd launched a new business but didn't yet know what it would do. My ten-year-old daughter had just earned her black belt in Taekwondo. And I moved my family from Arizona to North Carolina.

Selling my company brought many different emotions – gratitude for my good fortune, joy for my achievements, and relief about overcoming some tough challenges. There was also excitement, anxiety, and fear for where I was at that moment, and where I was heading in life. I was not just starting the next chapter of my life; I was beginning a whole new book. And right then, I was faced with a pile of blank pages.

It was during a visit a year before with an old high school friend that I realized how I wanted to fill those pages. During our conversation, my friend made several references to our "glory days" being behind us. At fifty-three years of age, I could not disagree more! I believe a better self is always possible today, and every day, for the rest of our lives.

I have been given so much; my next grand adventure would be focused on giving back. I would shift my focus from striving for financial rewards, prestige, and personal power to a more spiritual contentment of doing work I love and helping others. Studying the wisdom the great Dr. Wayne W. Dyer imparted had taught me that helping others improve their lives is more valuable than any amount of money. While driving from Albuquerque to Oklahoma City, I decided that from that day forward I would be guided by one simple mission; to improve the health and wellbeing of the world, one person at a time.

A BEAUTIFUL BUSINESS

Although I had been rewarded handsomely in the sale of my company, in truth, I didn't want to let it go. It perfectly fit every principle, outlined below, of my philosophy for lifelong work[24].

- It was work I wanted to do for the rest of my life.

- Its products and services could be broadcast to the world. It had no geographical limitations. (Like an e-book.)

- It had very highly recurring revenue. This means our customers paid for the products or services they used, every year. And would forever if they continued to get value in doing so. (Like car or homeowner's insurance.)

- Our products and services had near-zero marginal cost revenue. Once we created a product, we could sell it over and over again without incurring additional production costs. (Like an e-book.)

It was a company that filled a very important, and very distinct niche in the international trade industry. We turned the paper-based rules and regulations from each country into digital databases that our clients could use with their computer systems. We also created software and provided services that helped them accurately classify all their products from a customs perspective, for every country they purchased from or sold to. We fit the *Good to Great* hedgehog theory[25] of doing something you can be the best in the world at doing. I believe we were the best company in the entire world at our specialized niche.

We had an amazing staff and great leadership in every critical role. After nearly ten years, I told my investor group, "The most disposable of any of our top ten leaders are the two top executives; my partner and me." I meant, of course, that our team knew what needed to be done, and they did it.

Our customers were fantastic. They loved our products and supported us in the marketplace. The industry of international trade compliance was largely a group of true professionals who worked together in support of advancing the industry as a whole.

I loved the travel: We were doing business in more than twenty countries, and participating in industry conferences around the world. It was exciting to meet new people, learn about new cultures, and evangelize about our company all across the globe.

The business had an amazing growth record under our ownership.

In 2004, we acquired one company that specialized in digitizing the rules and regulations every country has for shipping products into and out of their territory. At the same time, I founded a start-up that would develop software and services to help companies create and maintain databases describing their products in the language of the customs requirements for every country they did business in.

In 2005, we acquired one of our suppliers. In 2006, we landed a major strategic partner. In 2007 and 2008, we developed and launched two software platforms. From 2009 through 2012, we continually optimized our technology, our processes and our teams. We focused on serving our customers' needs, growing our sales with existing customers, and expanding sales with new customers.

In 2013, we merged the two businesses into one. I stepped out of daily operations to become the Chairman of the Board. My partner and our team of great leaders were left to run the business. Throughout nearly ten years, we had an average annual increase in sales of 28.29%. Sales in 2013 were ten-times higher than 2004.

For the first three years, the businesses lost money. In year four, we turned the profit corner and never looked back. In the years that followed, our profit growth far exceeded our sales growth because of the highly recurring and near-zero marginal cost nature of its revenue, and due to the great work of the team members, who continually optimizing technologies and processes to get more work done with less cost.

Virtually all the profits from years four through seven were plowed back into operations and servicing debt. In year eight, we were debt free. We were highly profitable. We had a great management team, great products, and wonderful customers.

It was a beautiful business.

CREATIVE CONTROL

Two years later, in January 2014, amongst a great deal of political and unnecessary strife, I was the only board member of five who didn't want to sell. But I didn't have enough power to stop it.

Let me briefly take you back to the beginning to explain why.

The first week in January 2004, I was still working in the audit business. I had delivered my "Iconoclast" report to the CEO, but had not yet been fired. I spent three days in the Bentonville Audit Center working on optimizing the duplicate payment processes for the Wal-Mart audit. I had made plans to return two weeks later. As the return trip approached it was postponed by headquarters. Something was very suspicious. On Thursday, January 22, 2004 I was fired. Well, they couldn't actually fire me because I was a good employee with no fire-able offenses… but they could lay me off, and that's what they did.

On Friday, January 23, 2004 I started my own business.

My good friend, technology wizard Tom Jacobs had been fired right alongside me. He immediately joined me on my mission to offer the accounts payable recovery industry a better, more modern solution. Our new company would create products and services that empowered the customer. We would re-purpose our audit knowledge, technologies, processes, and services to enable our clients to modify their corporate systems and processes to reflect the full intent of the buyer (using automating auditing rules), and prevent errors from happening in the first place. I named the business Buyer$Intent.

Tom worked for me for free for nearly a year. His loyal and courageous gesture led him to a string of good roles with my companies from October 2004 until the end. As I write these words, he's employed for the company that bought us.

For his effort and unwavering support, I awarded Tom a percentage ownership in Buyer$Intent, so-called sweat-equity because he earned it through work rather than from the contribution of capital. The sweat-equity he earned in ten months of 2004 has paid him nearly $600,000 so far, with more to come.

By June, I had already taken a few business development trips in Colorado and Kansas, and was preparing for a two-week trip to prospect for customers in Northern California. A week before the trip, I received a phone call from a good friend in the auditing business. She said her husband was interested in buying a customs business. She wanted to know if I would invest.

Customs? I had heard the term before but I really didn't know what it meant. I thought it might have something to do with the financial sector. I didn't have any money. My last payday from my severance package had ended a few weeks earlier, so I wasn't planning to invest. But I was curious and decided to meet them to learn more.

So, on my drive from Colorado to California, I stopped in Salt Lake City, where my friend's husband pitched me on the customs business and I pitched him on Buyer$Intent. Neither of us was buying what the other was selling. However, for some reason, I was intrigued. I continued mulling over the customs business throughout the two weeks of my prospecting trip.

Lightning Bolt: Could there be a way to combine the customs business with the auditing business?

On my return trip I stopped again in Salt Lake City. This time I pitched my friend's husband on an idea to buy the customs business and launch a start-up company that would leverage the customs business and our auditing experience. He liked it. We agreed to become partners. He would lead the customs business and I would lead the start-up.

With that agreement, I completely abandoned all my plans for the auditing industry and immersed myself in learning a new industry of international customs compliance. I stayed in Salt Lake an extra day and we met with a potential investor. I returned two weeks later and we worked to get our ideas on paper, and to create a vision of what these businesses could become under our leadership. We met with the investor again. We had made enough progress that he was becoming interested. On August 11, 2004 we were all confident enough to submit a bid to buy the customs business. Nine days later, we won the bid. Now we had to figure out how to pay for it.

The next two months were a fury of activity. We worked through the due diligence to buy the company, prepared documents and presentations to raise the money, managed all the legal things, created the limited liability company structures for the two businesses, and perhaps most importantly, negotiated the terms of the deal between the operators (my partner and I) and the investors.

We needed $1.5 million to buy the customs business and another $1 million for start-up costs and on-going operating capital for both companies. The investor liked the deal. He and his Salt Lake City group wanted to invest. My partner and I wanted to retain control of the businesses. We hammered out an agreement. The Salt Lake City group would put in $200,000 up front and another $300,000 in the future (as needed) in exchange for a 20% ownership position. My partner and I would put in $500,000 for a 50% ownership position. We would raise another $1.5 million for the remaining 30%.

The way I figured it, the power of 50% ownership gave us creative control. It meant no one had authority to change what we were doing unless my partner or I agreed. It wasn't a perfect deal but I was happy enough. I was so certain of our success that I just wanted to get started.

Two major funding hurdles remained. Number one; we needed to have a business plan and vision impressive enough to raise $1.5 million in exchange for 30% ownership. Number two; I needed to come up with $250,000 of my own, which I didn't have.

Towards the end of September, we were ready to present the opportunity to outside investors. The Salt Lake City group had a network of angel investors they pitched deals to. They set us up with two meetings. The first, in Salt Lake City, went well enough that the representative invited us to Portland, Oregon to present the opportunity to his larger group. The other was a conference call with an investor in Chicago. It went so well that he offered to put in $500,000 for 10%. We were very pleased with that, but the meeting in Portland, one week later, went even better. They offered the entire $1.5 million but they wanted more than 30% ownership. We were unwilling to give a larger percentage, as we would lose creative control. So instead of buying in, they asked us to treat their $1.5 million as a loan.

We agreed. That meant the Portland group would get the first $1.5 million in profits and interest on their money before the rest of us received any return on our investment. I was so naively certain of our success I figured it would be just a few years. I had no idea it would take nearly seven years to repay the Portland "loan". We told the Chicago investor we were fully funded and moving forward with Portland. It took a major concession, but hurdle number one was done, and done fast. We had all the outside funding we needed to proceed.

Hurdle number two had suddenly become more interesting, and more challenging. My partner was only able to assemble $100,000. I offered to put in $400,000 in exchange for 37.5% ownership and he could put in his $100,000 for 12.5%. He accepted the deal. Now, I needed to somehow find $400,000, and fast.

Our business plan and vision had been strong enough to convince outsiders to invest in our business. I wondered, why not present an investment opportunity to family and friends? I created a limited liability company called G1 Management to be my investment company. G1 Management had, and still has two partners; me personally (Matt Gersper) and my business I had started to revolutionize the auditing industry (Buyer$Intent). I own one percent of G1 Management and Buyer$Intent owns ninety-nine percent.

I decided to sell shares of Buyer$Intent to raise investment capital from family and friends. I would use that capital to make investments from G1 Management. Our first investment would be for 37.5% share of the customs business and the start-up.

I parceled Buyer$Intent into shares, which I offered to family members and friends.

I designated all family and friends shares as financial-only interest in Buyer$Intent. Doing so let me retain operating control and complete decision making freedom within both Buyer$Intent and G1 Management. I was again pitching a business plan and vision, this time demonstrating the value of an investment in Buyer$Intent. I contacted everyone I knew who I thought would be interested and might have the means to invest. In a few weeks' time, I had sold enough shares in Buyer$Intent to raise the $400K needed to secure my investment in the customs business and the start-up.

The business structure has worked well for me and for my investors. To date, G1 Management has invested in five different businesses. Each of the initial family members and friends remain invested with me after nearly eleven years. They have received an average annual return of more than thirty percent from their investment, and the company remains invested in two promising businesses today, including the company that published this book.

BREAKNECK SPEED

We started official operations of the customs business and the start-up on October 29, 2004, only four months and eight days from my first visit to Salt Lake City.

The years to follow were the most creative of my life so far. I learned new roles. It was my first time as a business owner. It was my first time being an investor. I was the founder and top executive of the start-up. I served on the board of both companies. That was a lot to learn, but to make things even more challenging, I was beginning all these new roles in an industry I knew absolutely nothing about. It was a period of very rapid learning, under the fire of high expectations.

In the early years, I spent most of my time and energy in the start-up company. I really struggled to find its true identity. I think businesses are a lot like people in that way. People and business can do many things. With discipline and effort, they can be trained to do things well. But when you discover the thing a person or a business is *meant* to do, that's when magic can happen.

Our customs business already had its true identity. In the early 1990's, the company's founder created a service to make it easier for customs brokers and international trade attorneys to research the rules and regulations of customs matters. He started with a focus on the United States. He built his research library on microfiche[26].

Under our ownership, we expanded the library to include nearly every country in the world, and added to our customer base many large, multinational companies that were shipping products to and buying products from all over the world. We digitized the library so it could be researched with lightning speed on the Internet and automatically integrated into our customers' computerized business systems.

Our customs business was like an artisan. It woke every day knowing that it would continue to master its craft of making customs content easier for its customers to use. The start-up was more like a college graduate with an identity crisis. It didn't know who it was or what it was supposed to do. It was my job to figure that out, and fast, so that it stopped losing money.

It took us three years, with three or four different business models, and nearly $600,000 in business losses, to find our way. Our start-up would become a specialty software company focused on helping its customers manage and use large databases. These databases described their products with all the proper customs information and requirements for every item.

During this time, I established a communication method that worked well for our investors and for me. I made a point of giving comprehensive face-to-face business updates on an *inconsistent* basis, to eliminate expectation based on the passing of time. When I did communicate, I did it well. I prepared in advance, was fully transparent, and presented where we had been, what we had accomplished, and where we were going. I ended every meeting with our investors by thanking them for their support. This worked well for them because they felt informed and appreciated. It worked well for me because I only reported to investors when I had something important to say.

As the top executive of the start-up, my primary jobs were to discover the identity of the company, create the vision of its place within the industry, set the strategic direction, create the business plan, and hire great people to implement that plan. In the early years, all this was a full-time effort.

We found our identity as the years went by. I began shifting more and more responsibility to the three fantastic leaders I had recruited to join me. Soon they were running all the day-to-day operations. They didn't need my help. Our little start-up was becoming a well-oiled machine.

I began spending more time in my investor and board member role. I analyzed the operational and financial performances of both companies. I thought about a collective strategy and wondered how our two businesses could become better together. I started pressuring the operators of both companies to do more. I believed the businesses should become more efficient every year through a stated strategy of continuous process improvement.

INFO GURU

Let me take you back briefly to the summer of 2004 to explain the method I used to quickly become known as an "expert" in an industry I knew nothing about. I was introduced to a marketing program called Info Guru just before we began operations of the two companies. I had received one of those free introductory CDs that just show up in the mailbox. This one had looked interesting so I'd kept it. I brought it along with me on the business development trip I took from Colorado to California. It was the same trip on which I met my partner, and it all began.

The main message of the program was that most businesses used strategies based on a model manufacturers used for marketing their products. The problem was that most businesses in the United

States are service providers not manufacturers. The New York Times confirmed the point, stating that about one-tenth of Americans work in manufacturing, while service providers employ about six in seven of the nation's workers[27].

The marketing program posited that the way to market a service company is by its leaders becoming known as experts in their industry. It suggested doing this by writing industry papers, speaking at industry events, and teaching with webinars and workshops. We were service companies, not manufacturers. This program certainly applied to us. So, I had to figure out how to become an expert in an industry in which I had no knowledge or experience.

Soon after officially beginning operations, I started what would become nearly a decade-long journey to turn myself into an expert and thought-leader in the industry of international trade. My first step was to write and publish what is commonly referred to as a "white paper". A white paper is an *authoritative* report or guide informing readers in a concise manner about a *complex* issue and presenting the issuing body's *philosophy* on the matter. It is meant to help readers understand an issue, solve a problem, or make a decision[28].

I had a big problem. I wasn't an "authority". I didn't know anything about the "complexities" of international trade. In fact, I didn't know anything about the industry. I certainly didn't have a "philosophy" on any industry issues.

So I educated myself and, as for a philosophy, I created one. It took me about five months, during which time I interviewed lots of people (customers, employees, and anyone I could find with expertise). I wrote at least twelve different iterations of my first white paper. Eventually I finished and published, *The New Normal: Import Compliance & the Forces of Change, An Executive Overview*[29].

It was the first of dozens of papers I authored. My writing opened the doors to industry speaking opportunities. When I wasn't speaking or writing, I was planning, marketing, and presenting my vision of our business in online webinars. We would often have hundreds of people from all across the globe attend our webinars or listen to the recordings afterward.

I recall one conference in Toronto, Canada. I was working in our booth, talking to a prospect, when someone walked by and stopped. I had never seen this person before. She looked directly at me. She asked, "Are you Matt Gersper?" I replied that I was, and asked how she knew. Astonishingly, she had recognized my voice from the webinars.

And that is the story of how one random mail solicitation of an obscure and free marketing program gave me a strategic insight that ignited my ability to promote our companies by establishing myself as an industry expert. It's another example of how teachers appear when you need them, and how acting on things which catch your interest can really pay off.

COLLECTIVE INTELLIGENCE

I was able to present myself as an expert beginning with my very first white paper only because I used the collective intelligence within an entire network of people associated with our companies. I learned from them. I wrote down what I learned. And I went back to them to make sure I had learned it right.

I used this same iterative process of learning, writing, and verifying in all of my marketing efforts. It helped me become recognized as a leader in the industry very quickly. Gathering and leveraging the collective intelligence of our industry helped me present knowledgeable and timely papers, speeches, and webinars throughout the ten years we ran the businesses.

This technique had a wonderful collateral benefit. The experts that I sought out to help me became invested in the piece I was working on. They felt like they were co-creating the work with me, and they were. As such, they took pride in the finished product and helped to promote it throughout the industry.

I applied the very same approach to develop world-class products to help our customers do their work better. Our approach was to listen carefully to our clients. We visited with them, learned how they worked and discovered what their challenges were. We asked how they would set about solving those issues if they had unlimited access to their company's technology staff. Whenever we thought we could solve their problem, we got involved, and usually did. When we found that we couldn't solve their problem, we tried to suggest a service provider that could.

During one such visit with a big customer in Atlanta, our contact said she was trying to figure out how her imports compared to other companies they competed with. She wanted an analysis of how much her imports cost compared to the competition. I asked if she knew a source that gathered and maintained all imports into the United States. She said yes, opened her desk drawer, and handed me a computer disc. I asked her a few more questions regarding her vision for the analysis. She gave me permission to borrow the disc of all US imports. Just a few days later, we had created what would become our *Competitive Trade Benchmark* report.

It turned out that the source for the import data also contained an amazing amount of other data that could help our customers gain insight into their import and export operations. This unexpected opportunity to help one customer was the catalyst for a new product line we called *Xtreme Trade Intelligence Reports*™. It ultimately became a library of more than seventy different import and export analyses.

Our programming team was brilliant. Its members developed all our services and software in the same way. When we found a customer with a problem we could solve, we solved it. But we delivered their solution using a computer platform that we could sell to another customer with a similar problem. When we sold it to the second customer, we had the opportunity to learn more about the problem and add additional features.

We would then notify the first customer that their software has been upgraded with new features for no additional charge (our costs for developing the new feature was paid for by customer number two). When we found a third customer, we learned more, we re-iterated the software, and we notified all our customers using that software of the improvements.

In this way, the software we created was really developed by the collective intelligence of our customers. It was *their* software. It was made to solve their problems. And it worked exactly how they wanted it to work.

This method of iterative product development based on the collective intelligence of our customers had two collateral benefits. First, our products literally became a best-practice repository for solving complex processes in our industry. Second, and just as with my marketing technique, our customers became invested in the product we created for them. They felt like they were co-creating with us, and they were. As such, they took pride in the finished product and helped us promote it throughout the industry.

Tapping into the collective intelligence of our network paid enormous dividends. It helped me become recognized as an expert in an industry I knew nothing about. It enabled us to develop world-class solutions for problems we knew nothing about. And it made us a lot of supportive friends and customers along the way.

FLYING HIGH

The techniques I used for marketing and product development produced an avalanche of information and opportunity flowing to my desk, and my mind. It created a virtuous circle of creativity for me. For example, we would meet with a customer and discover a problem to solve. We'd collaborate with that customer and develop a solution to the problem. I would create marketing materials describing the problem and our solution to it. We'd host webinars to present the solution to others. We'd execute the solution and then sell it to more customers. Then we'd continuously improve the solution, selling to more and more customers along the way, and simultaneously expand our knowledge of the problem.

Often our solutions were ending where another service provider's solution was beginning. For example, our customers may have used our software to research the proper way to describe their items from a customs perspective. They would then send those descriptions from our software to another system they used for creating import or export documents.

This led me to begin expanding the circle of creativity to include strategic partners. We discussed how we could solve our mutual customers' problems even better by working together. We explored synergies and developed cooperative solutions. I would create marketing materials describing the business problem and our joint solution to it. We'd co-host webinars to present our solution together. Back in my days at the hardware store, Art Simon taught me that I was a "part of an intricate business system". I was expanding this important lesson beyond our companies to the customs compliance industry itself. This continuously expanding circle of creativity was like a fountain of opportunity for improving our products, expanding our knowledge, making connections with strategic partners, and building our reputation within the industry. In fact, this is how we developed a relationship with the business that eventually bought us. I was working with them on developing a collective vision for the future of our industry, and how our companies fit within it.

Perhaps the most valuable outcome of this virtuous circle of creativity was that industry vision. As our product line grew, and my knowledge of the industry expanded, and our relationships with synergetic partners strengthened, my vision for our industry and how our businesses fit within it continued to evolve.

When I wasn't creating, I was selling. I was pitching our industry vision and our role within it to anyone with a stake in our businesses. That included:

- Investors: so they better understood the financial opportunity.

- Employees: so they could each see how their smaller part supported the greater whole.

- Customers: so they could see how our businesses could help them work better.

- Strategic Partners: so they could see how we could provide better solutions together.

- Industry Leaders: so they knew everything we were doing to improve the entire industry.

- Industry Analysts: so they understood how our businesses fit within the industry.

By year five, we were flying high. Our year-over-year sales were up more than 50%, and our profits even more than that. Our customers where happy, and our investors were thrilled. Our key employees were developing into real leaders, and gaining recognition both inside and outside our companies.

Business was rewarding and fun.

HERDING CATS

I learned a valuable lesson the first time I drove a Jet Ski. My daughter Shea, who was then ten years old, was behind me, holding on tight to my life jacket. I wanted to show her how fast we could cover the same distance I had swam earlier in the day. From a resting position, in the middle of the lake, I asked her to start counting as I went full-throttle towards the rocky shoreline of our home.

She was counting. We were speeding across the water. She continued counting "sixteen... seventeen... eighteen" as I let off the power and turned sharply to the left.

I didn't know that I couldn't steer the Jet Ski without power. I moved the handlebars hard left but without power, the Jet Ski kept skimming straight forward. The counting turned to screams as my daughter and I crashed over rocks at the lake edge and halfway up the rock wall that lines our property. She was terrified. To my great relief, neither of us was hurt. The Jet Ski survived my ignorance with minimal damage, but was scarred enough to serve as a constant reminder of this lesson, and it took a long time to shake all the "what ifs" out of my mind.

The Jet Ski incident is a metaphor for a problem I had with my businesses: I didn't have steering power when I needed it most.

In year six, I started spending a lot more time analyzing the performance of both companies. By year seven, I had created our first business plan combining both businesses into a single strategic vision. The plan included:

- Vision (What are we building?)

- Mission (Why does this business exist?)

- Objectives (What will we measure?)

- Strategies (How will this business be built?)

- Plans (What is the work to be done?)

It included a variety of financial metrics including forecasts for sales, expenses, profits, cash, and receivables. It included inter-company agreements that defined how the businesses operated together. And it contained our marketing plan.

This was my first genuine effort to manage the businesses as one. It was the first time we could see the big picture in a single ten-page document. And it was the beginning of the end because it created such friction between my partner and me. He wasn't interested in managing the businesses as one, and I didn't have enough "steering power" to force it.

I had operational control as the head of the start-up, and oversight responsibility of both companies as a board member, but I didn't have voting control. Creating strategic change was more like herding cats than codifying a new direction with a business plan. I could define exactly what I wanted to happen but would then have to stand aside in the hope that all the cats went where I wanted them to go.

Towards the end of year seven, my partner had had enough of my interference and pushing to manage the businesses as one. He called a board meeting and expanded it to include all eleven owners. He did not share the agenda with me. He was planning a coup. He wanted to have what he called a "public divorce" that permanently separated the two companies, and under the most unfavorable terms for the start-up, too. It would leave him in total control of "his" business, and I would be left with the shattered remnants of the start-up that he considered "mine".

I let him speak for more than an hour while he made his case. When he was finished, I presented the simple case that we have been integrating these businesses more and more for nearly seven years now. We had shared many systems, and processes, and people. The industry and our customers knew us as a single company. Most importantly, for the ownership group in the room, I made the point that we would be worth far more to them as one company than we were as two.

The vote was ten to one; we would not have a public divorce. Quite the opposite, we would officially merge the two businesses into one.

In the following months, I pushed hard for the board to choose one leader and one vision. I organized a three-day workshop where all our operational leaders presented to board members who they were, what they did, and how it supported the overall operation of the two companies. It was a very impressive set of presentations from a team that had become top professionals in their respective fields.
The board members were extremely impressed. They agreed we had a beautiful business that was poised for growth. I pressed them. We needed a single leader to take the company to the next level. They had to choose my partner or me, or hire someone else.

But they wouldn't. Instead we concocted a compromise. My partner would become the CEO of the merged company but with limited responsibilities, primarily focused on customer-facing duties. I would assume the chairmanship of the company with expanded responsibilities primarily in the areas of finance and strategy.

Over the course of several months in the beginning of year eight, I organized the development of our business plan. With each step of the plan, I implemented a review and approval process with each board member. We didn't complete any part of the plan until we had gained unanimous agreement. By the end, we had an eleven-page Business Plan describing our merged company's vision, mission, strategy, organization chart, financial plan (targeted revenue, expense, and profit). It also detailed job descriptions for the Chairman of the Board (me), Chief Executive Officer (my partner), and Chief Operating Officer, established board committees (for greater board oversight), and set out specific next steps for the CEO, financial functions, Chairman, and the board committees.

By the end of March, the Board unanimously approved (with each member's signature) the merging of our companies and the adoption of the Business Plan. This was my second effort to manage the businesses as one. This time I had used a collaborative process to include every member of the board (including my partner) every step of the way. This time, I had the signed consent of every board member (including my partner) approving the Business Plan. This time, I had built in the "steering power" I needed to assure the company progressed according to "our" plan.

Even this didn't work. I think I put my partner under so much pressure to perform better that it irrevocably damaged our relationship. He knew I didn't approve of the job he was doing. Dysfunction at the top of an organization seeps down. It got so bad in the end that board members and employees felt compelled to choose sides. Perhaps if I had worked half as hard at cultivating our relationship as I did at analyzing the performance of the business, things may have been different. My partner likely feels the same way my older children do: "Unacceptable!" may be a word he only hears in his mind from my voice!

In January of year nine, it was decided that the company would be sold. I was the only board member who did not agree. There was another way forward that would have allowed me to pursue the vision of the company I had spent nearly ten years developing but I was unable to convince the other board members. Even in this final act I lacked the steering power I needed to get what I wanted most. The board agreed to sell our company with a vote of four to one. Although selling was against my better judgment, I must admit to a huge sigh of relief that three years of turmoil were coming to an end.

What a ride I'd had, though. My time as a businessman was an intensely creative period of my life, full of ups and downs, which had taught me so much, and had both hugely expanded the person I was, and was to be a springboard for the person I would become.

Returning to my three questions can help reveal what I learned and how I grew and developed as a person and a business owner during this phase of my life.

> WHAT?: Business ownership.
>
> WHY?: Creative freedom to develop and pursue my vision.
>
> HOW?: Create a vision of a future that other stakeholders (investors, employees, customers, partners) want to join.
>
> Result: Turned a $700K capital investment into a $42M return in ten years, and learned a great deal about leading organizations, the importance of relationships, and building profitable businesses.
>
> *Who I became*: An innovative, collaborative, ambitious, high-energy, and competitive (Type A[30]) businessman. I wanted to conquer the world of international trade by creating and selling my vision to investors, employees, customers, and the industry.

As you can imagine, I learnt a whole raft of life lessons during those ten years:

MBG Life Lesson: Relationships are as important as financial success to create an enduring business.

MBG Life Lesson: If a business idea isn't good enough to convince others to invest in it, it isn't good enough.

MBG Life Lesson: The way to market a service company is by its leaders becoming known as experts in their industry.

MBG Life Lesson: Collective intelligence is always greater than individual intelligence.

MBG Life Lesson: Be curious. Ask the next question.

MBG Life Lesson: You can't steer a Jet Ski without power, and you can't control the fate of a business without voting control.

MBG Life Lesson: Go deep into a specialty. Get a customer. Make them happy. Then repeat...

MBG Life Lesson: Find work you want to do for the rest of your life, with products and services that can be broadcast to the world, with highly recurring revenue, and near-zero marginal cost.

Chapter 9 - One True Love
(2007...)

"Others who broke my heart, they were like northern
stars pointing me on my way into your loving arms."
(Rascal Flatts, Bless the Broken Road[31])

The fateful night in 2007 that ended my marriage
marked a new beginning to the rest of my life. On
Tuesday, September 18, the day after that last huge
fight, my business finally sold a few big deals that we
had been working on. That evening I saw three
shooting stars while relaxing and reflecting in my hot
tub. Two of them were spectacular. I felt like the
Universe was sending me a message.

Over the next eight days I spent as much time as I
could with my dogs, Liberty and Justice, and my hot
tub. The following Wednesday, I moved into a little
condo and began living life on my own, for the first
time ever. Four weeks later, my soon to be ex-wife
served me with legal documents dissolving our
marriage.

I was released.

I had a deep awareness that this moment was a
unique opportunity for me. In my calendar I called it,

"My Fantastic Adventure". I drew a graph depicting a life that had been "good" for forty-six years, but that now had the chance to become "great".

I spent a lot of time reflecting on what I was supposed to be learning. I could make a fresh start. I was free to do and become anything I wanted. But what exactly was that?

I decided to take my time. To enjoy the solitude of living alone and throw myself into my work and my physical fitness. I slowly began paying closer attention to people, places and things that inspired me. These were signals or messages about what is truly important to me, deep in my heart. Paying attention and acting on what inspired me would lead me onto a new path... from a good life to a great one.

I didn't know how. But I knew that's what I wanted. A magnificent life!

YOUNG MOMS

I was traveling a lot at the time. Over the final three months of 2007, I traveled to Phoenix, Arizona... Palm Beach, Florida... Toronto, Canada... Salt Lake City, Utah... Seattle, Washington... Napa, California... New York City, New York... and Chicago, Illinois. One thing became clear. I was attracted to pretty women, and they were everywhere. Then I started noticing something more.

> *Lightning Bolt:* I was attracted to young moms. Everywhere I would go, a pattern would repeat itself. A woman would catch my eye, I'd turn and look, and she would be a pretty... young... mom.

My kids were grown and raised. I thought, "What the heck is going on with me, being attracted to young moms?" But... I insisted, I must pay attention to whatever attracts me. I was getting a clear message from the Universe. I just couldn't understand it yet.

DATA MINING

Towards the end of the year, I started noticing something else. Once my life changed, the way I saw the world also changed. Up to that point in time, I cannot recall ever hearing an eHarmony commercial. Suddenly, I heard them all over the place. They were on my car radio. They were on the TV. I started asking, "What the heck is eHarmony?"

When I found out, I thought, "I'm not going to join eHarmony. That's a cheap way to meet women. It's much better the traditional way; in a bar after a few drinks." After a while, though, I begin thinking, "Wait

156

a second, you're in the data mining business. You make a living using data to help your customers make better decisions for their business. That's all eHarmony is doing for people in their relationships."

I eventually convinced myself it was a good thing to do. So I joined eHarmony on Friday evening, January 18, 2008. In the registration process, they basically ask: "What do you want?" The data mining way of asking that question is: "What are your filters?"

So, I considered the question. What *did* I want? I wasn't sure I wanted to get married again. Remaining a bachelor seemed like a pretty attractive option for me. I could focus on growing my business, and spend more time exercising, hiking, skiing, and rafting in the beautiful Colorado Mountains. I was comfortable in my own company, had plenty of friends, and the previous three months of travel had convinced me there would be plenty of opportunity to enjoy the benefits of being an eligible bachelor, too.

If I were ever to get married again, I decided it would have to be amazing. I would only marry again if I found my "soul mate". I wasn't exactly sure what that meant so I Googled it and found this:

How to Find Your Soulmate [32]

Many people feel that there's one person out there who can enrich your life in a way that no one else can. If there's only one person in the world who can be your soulmate, what are the chances they live in your town, look like the people you grew up with, or even speak the same language? Your soulmate does not have to live in the same country or even the same hemisphere as you.

Be willing to span the globe for your true love.

> *Lightning Bolt:* That's what I wanted. I would happily remain an eligible bachelor unless, and until, I found my one true love.

That's what eHarmony could do for me. It could span the globe for my one true love. These were my filters.

> Age: I was forty-six at the time; I input a wide range from twenty-nine to fifty-one years old.

> Geography: Why would I care where she lived? I was willing to span the globe for her. No filters.

> Race: What would I care what her race was if I found my soul mate? No filters.

Religion: Why would I care? No filters.

Politics: Uugghh! Grudgingly... I decided, even with politics, why would I care what her political beliefs were if I found my one true love. After all, James Carville and Mary Matalin are making it work, I figured. No filters.

I basically did a filter-less search. If you were a living twenty-nine to fifty-one year old single woman in 2008, you came into my computer every night, with lots of others.

My filter-less approach created a lot of work. Hundreds of eHarmony women were flowing to me every night. I was working full-time in my business during the day and working full-time meeting women during the evening, looking at pictures, reading profiles, answering questions, and paying attention to what I was attracted to. It was taking all of the organizational skills I had learned through my career just to keep pace.

Ten days later, a pretty redhead, "Dani, from Camp Verde, Arizona" captured my attention. We very quickly worked through the compatibility questions and answers and began communicating "outside the system".

159

We were emailing and talking almost every day. It felt like a courtship of days gone by when a new couple got to know each other with their words alone. With each passing day, the excitement of writing to her, or "talking her home" from her work commute, grew.

Dani was also a young mom (interestingly!). Now, I love children, but I don't love it when they ride roughshod over their parents. When I'd been noticing cute, young moms, I'd also been witnessing a lot of wild children running amok and out of control. I didn't think I could pursue a relationship under those circumstances, no matter how wonderful the mom may have been.

If I had any concerns, and I did, about falling for a woman with two young children, Dani unknowingly removed any doubt during one of our talks. She was on the four-hour drive south to visit her mother in southern Arizona. It was another one of our long conversations. We were talking easily about everything, as always. Suddenly Dani broke off to speak to her daughter, who was also in the car. "What would you like me to do?" she asked her. "I am not in control of the sun. Close your eyes!" I asked what that was all about. She replied that one of her daughters was complaining that the sun was in her eyes. It was clear in that moment that Dani was in charge of her children, not the other way around. I breathed a big

160

sigh of relief at that – as with everything else so far, it appeared that we were on the same page about handling children too.

With every step of our long-distance courtship, the more I learned about this lady, the more I liked. She seemed to like me a lot too. It was time to meet up. We really wanted things to work out between us but, being realistic, we both knew that if we weren't physically attracted to one another in person, it wasn't going to. The chemistry had to be right.

She asked, "How are we going to do that? You're in Colorado and I'm in Arizona."

I replied, "Well, I'll just fly down."

After all, I was willing to span the globe for my one true love, what was a little flight to Arizona?

THE PICTURE

On February 22, 2008, I flew to Phoenix.

So, there I am, at the airport. Dani meets me as soon as I clear security. Although we've never seen one another before, we hug each other deeply, as if it were a reunion of lovers who had been separated for years. We hold hands all the way to the baggage claim area. It's a strange and thrilling feeling, holding hands with such an intimate familiarity. I look at her and ask:

"Is this weird?"

She replies; "Yeah, it's kind of weird."

But neither of us wants to let go, even to get my bags into the car.

And guess what? We rarely let go of each other's hands for the entire weekend.

The next day, Dani took me out to explore Sedona. It was my first time to visit this particularly beautiful part of the world, known for its vast array of red sandstone formations. We had driven up to a popular lookout point to get a good view of some of the famous red rocks. It was fairly crowded with people, so we stepped up on a rock to see over those in front of us. Dani was standing in front of me, resting her back against my chest. I had my arms around her waist. She was gently holding me close to her. We just stood there, holding each other, looking out into this beautiful view, happy to finally be together.

Suddenly, a woman approached us.

"Do you mind if I take a picture of you?"

"What?" I thought. "Did she misspeak? Is she interrupting my perfect moment with Dani to ask me to take a touristy picture of her?"

"Did I hear you right?" I replied.

"Yeah,' she said. "I've never seen a couple so much in love."

Dani and I looked at each other, thinking, "Man, this is crazy. It's our first full day together and we're giving off such a powerful energy that a complete stranger wants to take a picture of it!"

That was a strong signal that we may have found true love.

The picture sits in a featured place in my office.

There was barely a moment when Dani and me weren't in each other's arms or holding hands during the entire weekend. We had passed the physical compatibility test with flying colors!

WHIRLWIND ROMANCE

It was so very hard to leave Dani and return home. We wanted to be together. We couldn't wait. We started planning the next visit immediately. This time she would come to Colorado. For two full days, it would be just her and me, alone in my dumpy little condo. We created a theme for the visit. We called it *Cook and Bake*. I would do the cooking, and she would do the baking. We planned the menus ahead of time. We shopped together. We cooked, ate, and cleaned the kitchen together. We talked, slept, and even showered together, in a tiny shower meant for one.

It was amazing. We couldn't get enough. We wanted more time together. We started planning another visit immediately.

The next ninety days were a whirlwind of romance. I spent a weekend at her home, and met her daughters. We had the most incredible weekend in New Port Beach, California. She came to Colorado for another themed weekend, *Love Under the Stars*.

When we weren't physically together, we continued our long-distance courtship of words. It really was a wonderful way to get to know each other.

I first saw my beautiful "Dani, from Camp Verde, Arizona" on the eHarmony website on January 27, 2008. By April 13, we confided that we loved each other. By Father's Day (June 15), I knew she was the woman I wanted to spend the rest of my life with. Dani captured the moment I realized she was my soul mate in her poem simply titled, *My Matt*. This is a small excerpt:

> On Father's Day '08 during a walk through the vines
> He had a revelation... a feeling that entwines
>
> He said he's found his true love... what a wondrous thing
> Two lives together... making their soul sing

A POETIC YEAR

That first year, Dani and I were apart more than we were together. The love we had discovered in each other was so great it felt overflowing. These two factors conspired to have us express our overwhelming love using the old-fashioned, tried and true method of writing poetry.

During one of our early phone calls, Dani said something and I replied that she was cute. She said she didn't think of herself as cute. That was the inspiration that began what would become our year of poetry.

My Privately Cute Dani

We met on the net, and shared thoughts thru the written word...
Then we began sharing calls so our thoughts could be heard

She was just so sweet... I said she was cute during our calls...
But cute did not fit her image and it gave her pause

She's a thoughtful woman, and so considered my view...
Could it be that she is cute and that she just never knew?

She loves pink polka dots, and frilly lace...
But never in a public place

She has a big city job, with lots of responsibility...
Her co-workers and colleagues never see the part of her she's shown to me

We continued to talk and to laugh and share our charms...
Then we planned a "real" visit so we could be in each other's arms

As I came down the escalator, I knew in an instant I was right...
She was smiling and so cute... what a beautiful sight

After two days together, it became obvious to see...
The cuteness in her came out when she's with me

As we laughed and we talked, we considered her two worlds...
In the one she's a consummate professional, in the other a sexy woman and a cute little girl

These two worlds of Dani are separated by a powerful wall...
She says one side is for me, the other is for all

Dani's publicly private and privately cute...
That means lace for me and for others a business suit

My sweet Dani, it is an honor for me that you have let me into your private world

Dani responded with a beautiful poem of her own telling me how I made her feel cherished.

Cherished

He has been on the periphery of my
consciousness all day...
I have so many feelings to express... I have so
much to say...

He is affectionate... He touches me in very
caring ways...
He is tender when he's with me and he's kind
with what he says...

He's a gifted writer and has touched my soul
with his written word...
He has penned some of the most beautiful
phrases I have ever heard...

He is protective... He makes a safe place for
me to be...
When we are together I feel secure physically
and emotionally...

He is determined... He convinced me of my
private cuteness... a mighty feat indeed...
He gathered his facts... and relentlessly made
his case until I finally agreed...

He is confident with himself... He's happy and peaceful from within...
I am free to be me when we are together... my thoughts and feelings unguarded with him...

He is attentive...He's genuinely interested in what makes me Dani...
He's selfless in that he wants me to be all that I can be...

He makes me feel like a woman... I feel cherished when we're together...
In his arms my world's a wonderland ... like discovering hidden treasure...

I was caught by surprise 'cause I thought this was all about my feelings from the start...
But I've learned I am beginning to capture his heart.

On and on it went. I'd write another. She would respond. Our courtship of words captured in verse. It was wonderful.

Other titles included:

- *I Have Found Someone Special*

- *My Favorite Place*

- *My Matt*

- *My Valentine... forever and ever*

- *Banana Cream Pie...*

- *FMGP Project (The Future Mrs. Gersper Project)*

We had such fun with our poetry that we created the Poem Olympics. The author of the poem would read it to the other who would act as the judge. The judge would then score the poem on a scale of 1 to 10, with 10 being a perfect score.

I read *My Privately Cute Dani*. She gave me a score of 10.

She read her poem *Cherished*. I gave her a score of 11, along with the commentary, "I am completely in love with you."

Our prolific writing about our love for each other stayed private until the rehearsal dinner for our wedding. Our poetry was such an important expression of our love, we asked our dinner guests, our closest family and friends, to write a poem about the relationship they had with her, me, or us. Each person who wrote a poem read it during our dinner celebration. We also asked selected guests to read a few of the poems we had written to each other.

It was a deeply moving experience, an incredible celebration of love. It was a truly amazing evening.

9/9/09

So, here's the scene. One of the most memorable of my life... I'm dressed to the nines in a black tuxedo, with a light gray tie and matching vest. It is a warm Wednesday morning in Sedona, Arizona. I'm waiting patiently, hands cupped behind my back, in a beautifully groomed meadow on the grounds of the L'auberge De Sedona resort.

Just off in the horizon behind me, and framed in a clear blue sky, is an amazing formation of red rock simply known as Snoopy Rock. It truly looks like nature has sculpted the famous Peanuts pooch into the side of the mountain.

Around fifty others are gathered there too. To my immediate left are my mom and dad, dressed in their "Wednesday" best. Behind them are many of my closest family members and friends. Dani's mom is on my right in the featured chair of the bride's side.

Those who have gathered in support of Dani surround her.

Suddenly, music begins to play. A beautiful redhead appears and slowly walks towards me. This is the little one, Dani's six-year old daughter, Shea. She's carrying a white laced-basket, filled with white rose petals, dropping a few with each step. Following her is Dani's second daughter, Sydney. She is only three years old. She's smiling, looking around at all the people gathered there, and gently spreading her allotment of rose petals.

The girls take their place, in front of the bride's side. We all just wait. It is one of those amazing moments of anticipation.

Another redhead appears. This is the one I had spanned the globe to find. Now she stands just thirty feet away from me in her wedding gown, holding a bouquet of white roses. She looks absolutely radiant. She walks slowly towards me. She is as happy, as confident, and as beautiful as I have ever seen her.

When she finally reaches me, we turn slowly, together, side by side, facing Snoopy. It is there, in that meadow, in the witness of our loved ones, on Wednesday, September 9, 2009, at nine-0-nine in the morning (9/9/09, 9:09 AM), we exchange our vows to love and care for each other, forever.

I have found the one person out there who can enrich my life in a way that no one else can.

I have just married my soul mate.

BONUS BEAUTIES

Soon after I had moved in full-time with Dani, we discussed the role I would have in raising her daughters. I assured her that I was willing to do whatever she needed me to do to support her. I was willing be the quiet step-dad and let Dani continue to make all the decisions regarding her daughters and enact all discipline, etc. Or, I could be a full partner with her and we could raise the girls together. The decision was hers to make and hers alone. She chose the latter. She had been an only parent for a few years following the death of her first husband. She eagerly welcomed me as her equal partner in this most important responsibility.

And so that's what we did.

Following that conversation, I dusted off my "parenting young children" skills and began again. The girls were young enough that they accepted me easily.

Dani and I were incredibly aligned in our views on raising children. We began working together as a team… a mom and a dad working in unison.

Dani gave me a most amazing gift just before our first year anniversary. She asked me to drop the "step" in my role as dad. She wanted me to adopt her girls and make them ours.

What an honor. What a gesture of love. To this day it has been such a great privilege to love, play with, and sometimes discipline our beautiful girls, Shea and Sydney. It is a great responsibility of trust to raise them up as my second and third daughters. It makes me so very proud when they call me 'dad'.

GROWING OLD, HAPPILY

You're in my heart, you're in my soul
You'll be my breath should I grow old
You are my lover, you're my best friend
You're in my soul

I always liked Rod Stewart's song, You're in My Heart, but I never understood the third line of the chorus, "You are my lover, you're my best friend". I didn't understand it, that is, until I found my Dani. She is my lover and my best friend. She is my soul mate.

The final twenty-two words of my toast to my beautiful bride on our wedding day were these:

"Dani, from the day I first met you, I could finally imagine growing old... gracefully and happily with my one true love."

As you can see, what started out as a tentative idea of looking for love ended in a fairytale romance, an equal partnership between lovers and best friends, and an expansion of my beautiful family with the inclusion of my two darling daughters, Shea and Sydney. So, to return to my three questions, and their answers:

WHAT?: True love

WHY?: I wanted to share my life with the person who made my heart burst

HOW?: Willingness to span the globe for my one true love using eHarmony

Result: I found my redhead, married her on 9/9/09 at 9:09 AM, and got two more beautiful children to love, too. I can report that a lifetime devoted to my one true love is happily in progress.

Who I am becoming: A blessed, content, loving man who adores his wife and can imagine, for the first time, happily growing old with his best friend and one true love by his side.

MBG Life Lesson: Pay attention to and act on what attracts you.

MBG Life Lesson: Soul Mates exist.

MBG Life Lesson: Drop the filters. Go big for what you truly want.

Chapter 10 - Tao Man
(2011...)

"Tao smoothes our sharp edges, untangles the knots
in our lives and blends our brilliance with our dust."
(Lao Tzu)

I'll begin with a story:

> Alexander in India encountered some
> gymnosophists (literally "naked wise men")
> sitting in meditation in the sun on the banks of
> the Indus. Alexander's party was trying to get
> through the busy street, but the yogis had
> their spot and they wouldn't move. One of
> Alexander's zealous young lieutenants took it
> upon himself to chase the holy men out of the
> king's path. When one of the wise men
> resisted, the officer started verbally abusing
> him. Just then, Alexander came up. The
> lieutenant pointed to Alexander and said to
> the yogi, "This man has conquered the world!
> What have you accomplished?" The yogi
> looked up calmly and replied, "I have
> conquered the need to conquer the world."[33]

ALEXANDER THE GREAT

Alexander III of Macedon, commonly known as Alexander the Great, was a King of the Ancient Greek kingdom of Macedonia. Born in 356 BC, Alexander succeeded his father, Philip II, to the throne at the age of twenty. He spent most of his ruling years on an unprecedented military campaign through Asia and northeast Africa, until by the age of thirty he had created one of the largest empires of the ancient world, stretching from Greece to Egypt and into northwest India. He was undefeated in battle and is considered one of history's most successful military commanders[34].

Alexander and his massive army were conquering the world with overwhelming military force and cunning. What he encountered that day in India was the incredible power of a highly developed consciousness within the naked yogi.

In his book, Power vs. Force: The Anatomy of Consciousness[35], Dr. David Hawkins explains how leaders operating from lower levels of consciousness use force, instill negative emotions such as anger, fear, and apathy among their "followers", and ultimately drive the world into chaos, tyranny, and despair. Leaders operating from higher levels of consciousness wield a quiet power, instill positive

178

emotions such as peace, joy, and love among their followers, and ultimately lead the world into harmony. Years of research and scientific validation by Dr. Hawkins and his team have shown the scale of consciousness is logarithmic, meaning each incremental level represents a giant leap in power.

In our story, above, Alexander recognized the elevated power of the yogi's consciousness, and laughed with approval saying: "Could I be any man in the world other than myself, I would be this man here."[36]

I agree with Alexander.

When I read that story, I thought, "I like that. I want to be that."

> *Lightning Bolt:* I would love to conquer the need that I've seemingly had my entire life to conquer things: to conquer my body, to conquer the business world, to conquer, conquer, conquer, one thing after the next.

DAILY TAO WITH DR. DYER

My journey toward conquering the need to conquer things started when I discovered the Tao. My relationship with the Tao began on June 4, 2011. My beautiful Dani introduced me to some of Dr. Wayne W. Dyer's interviews and, for my fiftieth birthday, I bought his book, *Change Your Thoughts – Change Your Life: Living the Wisdom of the Tao*[37].

For some reason I didn't understand, I was instantly attracted to this book. The Tao Te Ching (Tao for short, pronounced "Dow") is a spiritual text of 81 verses that is attributed to Lao Tzu, a philosopher of ancient China. The best description of the Tao that I've ever read comes from Michael A. Singer in his book, *The Untethered Soul: The Journey Beyond Yourself*[38].

> No discussion of living life as a spiritual path is complete without addressing one of the deepest of all spiritual teachings, the Tao Te Ching. It discusses that which is very difficult to discuss, that which Lao-Tzu called "the Tao". Literally translated, this means "the Way". The Tao is so subtle that one can only talk around its edges, but never actually touch it. In that treatise, the very basis for the principles of all of life is laid down. It is a treatise on the balance of yin and yang, the feminine and the masculine, the dark and the light. You could easily read the Tao Te Ching and never understand a single word, or you can read it and tears could pour from your eyes with

every word you read. The question is, do you bring to it the knowledge, the understanding, and the basis for comprehending what it is attempting to express?

Dr. Dyer introduces one verse of at a time, reflecting on its meaning with a short essay about applying Lao Tzu's wisdom in our modern world. I read one verse and essay each day for eighty-one days. The first time I read them, I barely "understood a single word". Somehow I felt both inspired and confused. I remember thinking, "Wow, there's a lot there that I don't know," but it seemed important to me. In short, I was hooked.

Feeling like I needed to learn more, I immediately started reading it over again. The second time through, I read the same verse every day for a week. I would spend the week just trying to think what the verse revealed about me, and about my life and what I am meant to learn from it. This practice helped me understand more and more over time and reflect on how I could apply the Tao's wisdom to my life. More than four years later, I am on my fourth pass through the book and preparing for the fifth.

The Tao has given me a framework for reflection. Figuring out who I am and what I want during this life requires reflection. It requires deep thinking. It's a process of paying attention to WHAT I am attracted to, and then asking WHY. It's helping me discover my path. It's showing me how I can become everything I am meant to be.

UNLEARNING LIFE

The Tao is teaching me that I must unlearn much of what I was taught during the first fifty years of my life. For example:

> Verse 48: One who seeks the Tao unlearns something new each day.

> Verse 64: What he (the Master) learns is to unlearn.

This was one of those Tao ideas I simply couldn't understand in my first pass through the book. Over time, though, as I came to understand more and more, I think that the unlearning spoken of in the Tao is responsible for my biggest and most important transformation yet.

- I had been taught to *fight* for what I wanted from life. Unlearning is teaching me to *surrender* to what life has in store for me.

- I had been taught that *more* is always better. Unlearning is teaching me that *less* is more.

- I had been taught to trust my *mind*. Unlearning is teaching me to listen to my *heart*.

- I had been taught that success is *getting more*. Unlearning is teaching me that success means *giving more*.

- I had been taught to *push* against resistance. Unlearning is teaching me to recognize resistance and *flow* with it.

- I had been taught to be *hard*. Unlearning is teaching me to be *soft*.

- I had been taught to lead by using *force* to get others to do what I wanted. Unlearning is teaching me how to use quiet *power* to help others get what they want as I follow my own path.

Studying and reflecting on the wisdom of Lao Tzu and Dr. Dyer has created a profound shift within me. Forty years of competitive athletics and cutthroat business taught me to fight hard and become better than the next guy. I was constantly trying to force life to fit my desire for some future goal. Unlearning is teaching me to pay attention to the moment and accept life as it is.

By this process of unlearning, I'm shifting my Ikigai[39] (a Japanese concept meaning "a reason for being") from striving for outward success (money, trophies, accolades, celebrity) to the inward contentment of doing my work well and helping others. As Dr. Dyer teaches, "To touch someone's life is more valuable than any amount of money."

Unlearning has also made me more aware of the inner spirit that dwells within me. I quiet my mind and listen to my soul. I'm learning to trust myself enough to follow my heart wherever it leads me because it knows where my happiness lies.

DISCOVERING MY MAGNIFICENCE

Many years ago when I watched The Secret[40] for the first time, I was instantly attracted to a phrase in the movie, "I am magnificence in human form".

> *Lightning Bolt:* While the phrase was inspiring, I was also intimidated by it. Magnificence felt like too grand a description for me, almost boastful and arrogant. But long after finishing the movie, "I am magnificence in human form"

stuck with me. It resonated somewhere deep inside. It seemed really important.

Many years studying the Tao, reading other spiritual books, taking long hikes, and hours of thought later, that phrase has become the centerpiece for my philosophy on spirituality[41].

I define spirituality as discovering and cultivating the inner being that is my unique soul. Spirituality is learning to detect the differences between energy and ideas created by my mind and those generated deep within my awareness. Spirituality is realizing that my inner spirit is my direct connection to the greater magnificence of everything, the Universe, the Almighty.

My spiritual practice is based on slowing down, being quiet, and listening to my heart.
The heart-based way (the path I want to follow or I am meant to follow) connects me to my spiritual source. Listening to my heart brings me energy, ease, joy, and grace. From this path I see abundance and feel generosity.

The heart-based way leads me into a world of personal power and harmony.

The head-based way (the path society says I should follow or that others tell me I am supposed to follow) connects me to the selfishness of my ego. Listening to my head brings me insecurity, worry, and shame. From this path I see a world of scarcity and I feel a need to protect what's mine.

The head-based way holds me in the world of force, chaos, and despair.

My spiritual practice is to recognize head-based thoughts (coming from outside me) and actions, and then replace them with heart-based ones (coming from within me). When I do this, energy, ease, joy, and grace flow into my life.

The Untethered Soul[42] helped me understand why the heart-based way allows the flow of happiness, and deep spiritual connection. Using the analogy of a pendulum, the author explains how the ego or mind-based path creates unproductive energy that pushes and pulls from one extreme to the other.

Bad thoughts, poor choices, and negativity create energy that forces the pendulum off-center. For example, breaking your diet one day, then feeling guilty and starving yourself the next. Telling a lie to gain something today, then getting caught and suffering consequences tomorrow. Skipping exercise one day, then going twice as hard the next and injuring yourself. Every push in one direction creates energy of equal force that swings back in the other direction. My pendulum sways off-center when I listen to the selfishness of my mind — and it doesn't feel good.

There is no swinging from side to side on the heart-based path. Energy is not wasted recovering from bad thoughts or poor choices. The pendulum stops swinging and instead energy moves forward unencumbered. This is why I have more energy when I follow my heart. My pendulum comes to rest at the center where there is no energy pushing me one way or pulling me the other.

I stay on-center when I listen to my heart and connect to something greater. When I am on-center, I feel energy, ease, joy, and grace.

When I am on-center, I may get into "the zone" [43] as my most creative self - immersed in an interesting project, losing track of time, and performing with ease.

Sometimes being on-center manifests as a powerful feeling of gratitude when I'm hiking alone in the natural beauty of wilderness. Sometimes when I meditate, a wave of emotion washes over me as I feel a deep connection to something greater than myself.

When I am on-center, I am living from the inner spirit that is my unique soul. I recognize and release energy or ideas created by my ego, and instead focus on those generated from within my deeper awareness.

When I am on-center, I cultivate my connection with the greater power of the universe. When I am on-center, I have incredible energy, my days are easy, and my life is full of joy.
When I am on-center, I am magnificence in human form — and it feels great!

UNDERCOVER TAO

In the summer of 2014, a friend emailed me a link to a video. It was an interview celebrating the 100th anniversary[44] of the founding of our football program at U.C. Davis. I sat on my back porch, overlooking our beautiful view of the lake, and reminisced about my time as a college football player.

I was surprised at how emotional I became watching the interview, seeing my old coaches talk about the meaning of Aggie football and Aggie pride. I began reflecting how much these men and the culture they created had influenced the trajectory of my life. It made me ask myself, "How significant was my time as

188

an Aggie in shaping the man I have become?" A few months later, I decided to find out. I interviewed my coaches and wrote an article called Something Significant: One Simple Thing – The Legacy of U.C. Davis Football[45].

It was great fun interviewing the three coaches. Coach Biggs had been the receiver's coach during my time at Davis. He and I developed our relationship while he was the team's head coach, long after I had moved on. Coach Foster had been the defensive coordinator during my years. He'd had the biggest impact on me as a player. Watching the video brought back great memories of the admiration and respect I held for him. My interviews with Coaches Biggs and Foster confirmed what I thought I knew about these impressive men: they were men of character, of commitment to excellence, and of selfless dedication to the program and their players.

It was Coach Sochor's interview that surprised me. He was the head coach during my playing days, and of the three coaches, I knew him the least. The longest period of time I had spent with Coach Sochor was during the dinner we'd had at my parents' house when he came to recruit me to the team during my senior year in high school. Beyond that, I had very little interaction with him so, I guess, I really didn't know him. I did know he was a very accomplished man, and highly deserving of my respect. I was anxious to meet him again, and I was intrigued about what he might tell me.

As Coach Sochor spoke, I was shocked to learn that the Tao Te Ching had strongly influenced his coaching philosophy. He confided that it was a foundational guide for how he coached. In the late 70's and early 80's, an enigmatic, eastern philosophy wasn't exactly accepted in the rough and tumble world of sports, let alone the physically violent game football. It would be another fifteen years before Phil Jackson wrote his national bestseller, *Sacred Hoops, Spiritual Lessons of a Hardwood Warrior* [46].

Coach Sochor felt compelled to translate all his messages and lessons in a way his coaches and players could understand, and accept. As far as I know, he never, ever mentioned the Tao. Looking back now, I see the groundbreaking experiment he tried, and the great risk he took. He was determined to lead a college football program using quiet power rather than force. He believed he could lift an entire football team to a higher level of consciousness, and therefore create a giant leap in its power.

Well, his belief paid off. His approach worked on the team. Coach Sochor served as the head football coach at the University of California, Davis from 1970 to

1988, during which time he compiled a record of 156 wins, 41 losses, and 5 ties, and won 18 consecutive conference championships, then a college football record[47].

It also worked on me. During my interview with Coach Sochor all these years later I suddenly understood why I had been so instantly attracted to the Tao upon buying Dr. Wayne W. Dyer's book. For four years, during my time as a football player at U.C. Davis, I had unknowingly been a student of it. As I poured through the book, it felt so familiar. It felt so *right*, somehow. It felt like coming home.

It is clear to me now that the innovative culture Jim Sochor created, and that I immersed myself in during my college years, has greatly influenced my personal evolution, and has had a big part in the creation of the man I have become today. At Happy Living, we published our first book in January 2016. It's called *The Belief Road Map[48]*. In our book, we teach our readers how to know themselves better and help them create personal philosophies to guide the way to the life of their dreams. It was my honor to dedicate the book to the memories of Coach Jim Sochor and Dr. Wayne W. Dyer. They are two men whose teaching of the Tao Te Ching has had a dramatic and very positive influence in shaping the philosophies of my life, and two men to whom I shall be forever grateful.

AVOIDING EXTREMES

I have long believed that it's easier to maintain order than to correct disorder. This is the secret of the middle way. I am happiest when I live my life in an orderly manner. When things get disorderly, it takes lots of extra energy to put them back. Disorder keeps the pendulum energized.

As Michael Singer describes it:

> The pendulum can swing all the way from gorging yourself to death, to starving yourself to death. Those are the two extremes of the pendulum: the yin and the yang, expansion and contraction, nondoing and doing.

> Everything has two extremes. Everything has gradations of this pendulum swing. If you go to the extremes you cannot survive[49].

Life has taught me that I have more energy and I am happier when I focus on my priorities, maintain order in my life, and avoid extremes.

The Tao is teaching me to accept life as it is in the moment. It's teaching me to trust in its framework of life lessons. I am learning to stop fighting, stop resisting, and let life happen. That's where I find quiet power, contentment, and happiness.

For my entire life I have been so focused on trying to conquer some future idea of my world. The Tao is helping me conquer my need to conquer the world.

Now, back to my three questions and my answers to them, as they relate to my study of the Tao:

> WHAT?: The spiritual teachings of the Tao Te Ching.

> WHY?: It provides a framework for exploring who I am and what I want deep within my heart.

> HOW?: Daily study of the Tao and reflecting on what it means in my life.

> Result: A lifetime of practice is in progress... *Who I am becoming:* A quieter, more content soul, focused on enjoying the moment rather than conquering some imagined future.

> *MBG Life Lesson:* To touch someone's life is more valuable than any amount of money.

> *MBG Life Lesson:* Don't resist life. Accept it as it is. It's the only way it can be.

> *MBG Life Lesson:* Stress is caused by non-acceptance of life. Clinging to a notion that

things *should be* different creates damaging stress in the body and mind.

MBG Life Lesson: It's easier to maintain order than to correct disorder.

Chapter 11 – Happy Living
(2013...)

"Live long. For you have gathered wisdom unique to
yourself, and the people still in darkness need the
light you have."
(Deng Ming-Dao[50])

It's taken me an entire lifetime to get here.

It's perfect summer weather for the last day of June
2014. I'm anchored in a secluded little cove on a
beautiful lake sipping my coffee, wearing swim trunks,
a t-shirt and flip-flops. From this place I'll write my
very first post for my next business venture. I'm sitting
comfortably on my floating office, a pontoon boat
Dani and I named *The Happy Living*. This moment is a
lifelong dream come true.

In Portland, Oregon, nearly one year earlier, I invited a
high school friend, Kevin Cady, and my son Kyle to
dinner. We enjoyed wonderful seafood at a
downtown restaurant. Kevin is an accomplished and
healthy man, married to the woman he loves, raising a
beautiful son they worked very hard to have. He has a
good job as an executive for a thriving construction
company. They own their house. But he must have
said a dozen times during our dinner, "You know, Kyle,
your dad's and my glory days are behind us." Yes, this

was the friend, with his "glory days" comment, that I mentioned in Chapter 8.

It really caught me off guard.

After dinner, I walked him to his car.

I told him how his repeated "glory days" comment bothered me. I couldn't disagree more. I felt nearly completely the opposite. In my early fifties, I felt like I was just coming into my own. I felt like I had more personal power, more things to do, and more resources to do them with (financially, spiritually, and from a half century of life experience) than at any previous time in my life. My "glory days" lay clearly in front of me, not in my past.

Luckily, being a great friend, he wasn't offended by me questioning what he said. In fact, he took it really well, and told me that my comments reminded him of a book he'd recently read called *Halftime: Moving from Success to Significance* [51], by Bob Buford. His office was only a few blocks away, so we walked up and he gave me his copy of the book. I thanked him and we said our goodbyes. But the evening stuck with me. I began wondering why and when people in general begin to feel that their best living is behind them. And I wondered why I thought differently.

A few weeks later, I embarked on my second annual solo hike down the Grand Canyon. I hiked about seventeen miles across the top and down the canyon on the first day. I ate, rested, read, and slept in the canyon at the famous Phantom Ranch[52]. The next morning I hiked the ten-mile trail out, climbing over a mile in elevation.

When I get out on solo hikes, I use them as opportunities for challenging my physical fitness and nurturing my spiritual fitness with nature and solitude. I also often set a problem I want to solve so an answer comes to me as my mind relaxes around it. And when I am not hiking, I read. This hike's book was *Halftime*.

The year before, my focus had been set around how to resolve the dysfunction brewing with my partner, our board, and how to successfully lead our trade companies. This year my focus was on my friend Kevin and his "glory days" comment, moving from success to significance as outlined in *Halftime*, and if there was anything I could do to help others shift their thinking from Kevin's perspective to mine. What a difference a year can make!

> *Lightning Bolt:* I left the canyon after two days in deep thought with a powerful inspiration to do something significant with the rest of my life.

READY, FIRE, AIM

Two weeks later, I invited my daughter Kaileen to visit for a weekend. I had a business proposition for her.

I met her at the curb of the Phoenix International Airport just outside of baggage claim. I grabbed her bag and gave her the key to my truck. It was a ninety-minute drive to my home in Camp Verde. I had a lap full of notes, ideas, and plans for my next business. I was hoping to explain my vision while she drove, and persuade her to join me in making it happen.

First I told her about Kevin's "glory days" comment. I explained the important concepts I had learned while devouring *Halftime* at the bottom of the canyon. Bob Buford's message was like a spiritual *Good to Great*. He says we spend the first half of our lives doing what we are supposed to do: i.e. getting educated, getting a job, getting married, raising a family, and building a successful life. Then we hit half time. The kids leave the house. Our jobs no longer inspire us. We look towards retirement resting on first half accomplishments. That's how many people in the wealthy West go about life and that's what my friend Kevin sounded like during our dinner in Portland.

There are some people, Buford says, who, upon reaching half time, find a good-to-great-like inflection point. In other words, they feel a pull to do something more. They have a spark inside them, a calling to do something important in the second half of their lives. Of course, the first half may have felt very important, stimulating and satisfying too. Even if that was the case, there is still the opportunity to reach for more in the second half. Some lucky ones may begin fulfilling their creative purpose from the outset. Still, everyone can apply all the skills they've acquired in the first half to something truly significant in the second.

The "retirement" group has an arc of creativity that rises during their first half as they do everything that is expected of them to be a responsible citizen in our modern society. Then half time comes. They breathe a sigh of relief. Then they spend the second half with their arc of creativity steadily diminishing until they die.

The "other" group has a similar arc of creativity in the first half. Then half time comes. Rather than a sigh of relief, they're stirred by an unfulfilled calling. A strong sense of commitment and excitement overcomes them to become all that they are meant to become. Their arc of creativity explodes as they begin a life-long practice of discovering and mastering their personal calling. If they're lucky, they die putting the final brush stroke on their masterpiece of life.

> *Lightning Bolt:* That's what I wanted. I wanted to spend the rest of my days working on my personal calling, and helping others to discover theirs.

That evening Kaileen and I sat on the patio continuing our discussion. Dani joined us. I began pitching them on my thoughts for launching our new business. We would help people discover their calling and follow their destiny all the way to mastery and magnificence. We would espouse that every person can improve every day with a rigorous practice of discipline to his or her craft. We'd inspire people to lead a vigorous life into old age. We'd create a health and wellness company akin to the grueling, ultracompetitive conditioning programs like CrossFit.

I'd beat the drum and shout, "Get happy forever!"

I finally ran out of breath and noticed the looks on my wife and daughter's faces. They were horrified. They said in unison, "You will scare people. You're scaring us right now." They quickly convinced me that my ideas were "a bit" (i.e. a lot!) too hard-charging, but they were also certain that the general idea was a good one.

So, we tossed out the harsh concepts of "rigor", "vigor", and "ultra-discipline" replacing them with "significance", "love", and "happiness". They talked me off the ledge of "extreme happiness" into the softer and gentler idea of "happy living".

Yes. Happy Living.

In a lightning bolt moment, we knew that that should be the name for our new company. I asked Kaileen if the URL happyliving.com was available. After a quick search she gave us the good news and the bad. Yes, the site was available but... it cost ten thousand dollars... Ten grand for an empty website!

We had no business plan. We had nothing but my head full of random ideas about improving health and wellness. Still, without so much as a blink of an eye, my wonderful wife pronounced Happy Living the perfect name for a gentler, more accessible version of my idea to help others get the most meaning and joy from their second half.

I gave Kaileen my credit card. We bought the URL right then and there.

MASTERPIECE

At that time, I was only six months into my new role as chairman of the board for our newly merged trade company. My plan was to slowly transition myself out of any day-to-day responsibilities, into a truly oversight role requiring just a few days a month. When I had begun my chairmanship, I'd known I wanted to start some kind of new business venture. Now I knew what it was, and I owned expensive real estate in the World Wide Web to build it on.

The trade company would keep me working a fulltime schedule until the day we sold it nine months later. Whenever I could find time, my thoughts turned to Happy Living. How would we help others believe, as I did, that every person has a calling, their own special gift to the world? I began writing down thoughts and ideas as they came to me. These eventually became my outline for a simple business plan.

On January 9, 2014, I invited Kaileen back to Camp Verde. This time I presented my business plan. They included stealing her from her current employer to join me as an owner of Happy Living. Much to my delight, she accepted.

> *Lightning Bolt:* The following week, reading in my comfy chair before starting my workday, an inspiration struck me that would shape the trajectory of the rest of my life.

I captured the moment in the following note to myself. I signed it to make it official.

> January 16, 2014

> During my morning reading, I had a very strong feeling "come over me" that Happy Living is to be the Masterpiece of my life - my personal and unique gift to the world.

I am committed to selling the international trade business and dedicating my professional time and resources to building Happy Living into a successful company that helps people lead happy, healthy, and extraordinary lives.

Matt B. Gersper

Matt Gersper

That was the moment I stopped fighting my board and prepared to move on. A few weeks later, we accepted an offer to sell the trade company.

HALFTIME

My personal halftime, the good-to-great inflection point of my life, came during my week of reflection in my hot tub following the last big fight that ended my first marriage. Six years later, in the bottom of the Grand Canyon, I realized that Bob Buford's book fit me like a glove. The more I read, the better it fit, too.

It provided a framework to describe the path I was taking to change my life from good to great. It activated a spiritual energy within me. It helped me understand the lightning strike of inspiration that had hit me on January 16, 2014. It gave me increased confidence to listen to that inspiration.

The book *Halftime* challenges its readers to reflect deeply about what is truly important to them. Bob

Buford asks the reader to choose the *one big thing* that's the most important to their life. Not two things, not three, or four, but the one big thing.

To assist the reflection exercise, he suggests writing your own *epitaph* and the *mission* for your life.

These were extremely difficult and personally invigorating assignments for me. It took months of mental and spiritual contemplation to complete. Ultimately my answers act like guiding lights on my path from good to great.

> My one big thing: The Tao.
>
> My epitaph: My life is my message.
>
> My Mission: Improve the health and wellbeing of the world, one person at a time.

In order for me to help others lead a happier, healthier, and even extraordinary life (my professional work), I had to also figure out what that meant for me (my personal work). I had to dig in deep to discover who I was and what I wanted. So I asked myself the following questions:

- What am I really good at?

- What do I want to do?

- What is most important to me?

- What do I want to be remembered for?

- If my life were absolutely perfect, what would it look like?

In my figuring out process and my struggle to answer the questions, I came to a clear understanding of the biggest question of all: Why am I here?

I believe I am here to become all I am capable of becoming with the gifts I've been given so that I am able to give to others, and in turn help them to become all they are capable of becoming with the gifts they've been given.

With this realization, choosing my *one big thing*, writing my *epitaph* and my *mission* for life became easy.

The Tao is my *one big thing* because it is my path to becoming all I am capable of becoming.

I chose "My life is my message" for my *epitaph* to reflect an attitude of allowing rather than interfering, and of sharing rather than advising. I cannot presume to know the best route for another's journey to their absolute best life but I can share what I am doing on my journey.

My *mission* for life is "to improve the health and wellbeing of the world, one person at a time" because that is my way to give to others, and help them become all they are capable of becoming with the gifts they are given.

That's the mission for my personal and professional life. It's my reason for being here. It answers the call to do something significant with the rest of my life.

It's how I am creating a great life in my second half.

INSPIRATION

The biblical idea of "to whom much is given, from him much will be required"[53] is one of the driving forces behind Happy Living. I have worked hard to create a good life for my family and me. I believe in pursuing happiness and living successfully in my life, without arrogance and without apology.

I also acknowledge the many blessings I have been given: loving and supportive parents, a college education, and sufficient health, intellect, and personal talent to contribute to society. Perhaps my greatest blessing was being born in America where I have the freedom to pursue my dreams and become whatever I am capable of becoming.

I have been given much. Now, I feel, I have the opportunity and responsibility to give back to others.

The "glory days" conversation with my friend Kevin, the inflection point of *Good to Great*, the big questions from *Halftime*, and a lifetime of "feeling" successful swirled in my mind as I searched for "how" I could give to others.

I began exploring my life - wondering why I have always "felt" successful, often in spite of evidence to the contrary. My life has been full of ups and downs, successes and failures. "Why do I feel my best days lie ahead of me?" I asked myself. "What causes my friend to say his glory days are behind him?"

As I explored, I noticed a pattern. I saw that I have developed a persistent willingness to say YES to opportunities for self-improvement.

Improvement requires change. Change invites risk. Risk creates fear of failure, embarrassment, losing money or friends, or even worse. No matter what my circumstances have been, I have always been willing to change, and take action in spite of uncertainty.

Cultivating a persistent willingness to say YES has led me on incredible adventures that I never could have imagined. Practicing self-improvement as a way of life has led me on a crazy journey of ups and downs, highs and lows, good times, and bad, as I continue to explore and experiment with life. I have never ended up where I expected to go, not exactly. But each adventure enriched my life. Each step helped me grow. Every turn seemed to reveal new opportunities, many of which I was not able to see before. It's incredibly uplifting knowing that there is always, and will always be, something I can work on to improve.

That's why I feel my best days lie ahead of me.

The strong feeling that came over me on January 16, 2014 was my answer to how I can give back - by helping others to realize that a better self is always possible today... everyday... for the rest of their days.

That's the purpose of Happy Living.

ROAD MAP

Inspiring others to embark on a virtuous journey of self-improvement is not enough. It may provide motivation for WHAT they want but leaves unanswered the question of HOW they can get it. So, to try and find out, I began asking how I found it in my own life. What tools did I use to cultivate my personal health and wellbeing?

I wanted to find a road map that would help others on the path to their absolute best life. While pondering this, I discovered a framework I use to prioritize my life. Think of it as the highly personalized filter I use to decide what is important to me, and what is not. These are the things that I decided were important.

- Doing what I must to meet my basic needs and care for my family.

- Doing what I love to expand my life and become all I am capable of becoming.

- Making my contribution to the world by helping others bring more health and wellbeing into their lives.

Health and wellbeing is more than keeping my body free from disease. For me, it's a daily practice. It's my life-long journey to make continual improvements in what I call my Seven Foundations of Health. These are:

- Physical Fitness

- Mental Fitness

- Spiritual Fitness

- Financial Fitness

- Love

- Adventure

- Significance

Physical Fitness is what might first come to mind when thinking about health, and I believe it is crucial to maintain the health of our bones, muscles, and organs. Physical fitness includes exercise[54], nutrition[55], and sleep[56], as well as important health maintenance like diagnostics, blood work[57], and doctor's visits.

Mental Fitness is often referred to as mental health. Even though it's not as "tangible" as physical fitness, it is just as vital. In addition to caring for mental illness, mental fitness includes reading[58], meditation[59], goal setting[60], creativity, lifelong learning, and the pursuit of hobbies.

Spiritual Fitness is the connection between our inner self [61] and something greater. It can be faith-based, found through meditation, or observed through science. It can be cultivated within a community or alone. Discovering and cultivating the inner spirit is what energizes the Power of the Heart.

Financial Fitness is being able to provide for oneself and for others. It includes living within one's means, in alignment with one's priorities, and in way that does not put financial strain on savings. It is becoming informed, educated and responsible with personal finances[62], and giving[63] to others when possible.

Love is essential to a healthy life. It breathes peace into hectic moments. It helps us persevere through tough times. It gives meaning to relationships. It

210

pushes us to pursue our passions. Self-love[64] is just as important to Happy Living as loving others. Without it, we cannot give our best selves to those around us or to the work we do. Love provides us with purpose, happiness, and joy.

Adventure is not just about being extreme. It's a spirit of being open to new possibilities, embarking on unchartered territory[66], and welcoming new discoveries[66]. Adventure can happen close to home or far away[67]. It can be a state of mind or an epic getaway[68].

Significance [69] is the big secret to happiness and good health. We add meaning to our lives through the pursuit of significance. It translates into a daily practice in prioritizing those things that are most important. Significance is dedicating your time, work, and life to something of great meaning to you, and that provides value to others.

These Seven Foundations of Health are at the heart of my personal and professional work to become all I am capable of becoming, so that I am able to give back and help others become all they are capable of too.

These foundations serve as a road map of personal beliefs[70] I rely on to guide my life. I want to take this opportunity to reiterate that I do not presume to know the right map for *your* best life. Or for anyone's best life apart from my own, for that matter. My intention and hope in sharing my road map with you is that it may serve as a template so you can develop one that's just right for you.

TRAIL MARKERS

The journey to your best life is long. The road often presents obstacles that are hard to overcome. The right path to choose is sometimes difficult to see.

At Happy Living we leave trail markers on our path in hopes that it will help others, whom may choose to follow a similar route. We research, experiment with, and write about concepts, products, and resources that promote *our* health and happiness so we can share what we learn with others. These weekly blog posts and best practices are intended to provide comfort when the journey feels long, motivation when the road is hard, and information when the path is difficult to see.

Our weekly posts are derived from our own personal experiences and from a handpicked team of Happy Living experts who are dedicated to sharing ideas for happier, healthier living.

My great hope is to provide inspiration, a road map, and trail markers to help at least one person improve their health and wellbeing, and then another, and another... until together, we have improved the health and wellbeing of the world.

So, it's time to return once again to my three key questions, the results their answers brought me and the life lessons those results yielded to me. Here, of course, we will look at them in relation to HappyLiving.com.

WHAT?: Improving the health and wellbeing of the world.

WHY?: It touches a deep sense of responsibility within me to give back and help uplift others.

HOW?: Researching, experimenting, writing and speaking about concepts, products, and resources that promote health and happiness.

Result: HappyLiving.com and my lifelong commitment to help others lead a happier, healthier life are in progress...

Who I am becoming: A writer and motivational speaker focused on inspiring others to lead their absolute best lives.

MBG Life Lesson: Live life without arrogance and without apology.

MBG Life Lesson: Develop a persistent willingness to say YES to opportunities for self-improvement.

MBG Life Lesson: Practice self-improvement as a way of life.

Chapter 12 - Lake Man
(2014...)

"Make your heart like a lake, with a calm, still surface,
and great depths of kindness."
(Lao Tzu)

For as long as I can remember I have wanted to live
"on the water". Whether it's a stream or river or lake
or ocean, the water has always had a calming,
peaceful, almost spiritual effect on me. I discovered
that living on the water had also been a lifelong
dream of Dani's, too, and we decided to try it on. So, I
want to rewind for a moment from where I left this
story, with me making the four-day drive down to our
new lake house in North Carolina, and fill in some
details about how we turned our initial inspiration, a
deep shared desire to live by the water, into action,
and fully realized our dream.

In July 2011, Dani and I rented a lake house for two
weeks, the longest vacation either of us had ever
taken. The rental house was a shabby little
doublewide trailer with a lakeside bonus room added
on. The property had about one hundred feet of
shoreline and a private dock.

We explored what it would be like to live in a lake
house. We ate most of our meals at home. I grilled on

the patio most every night. Often, I worked in the mornings, and I swam in the lake every day for exercise.

We played on the lake. We watched fireworks on the Fourth of July from "our" dock. We rented a pontoon boat for three days. The girls swam and played with a cute little dog named Pebbles. She was the rental owner's dog (who lived next door), and she came over to play every day.

On the middle weekend, Kaileen and her fiancé came to visit. We loved every minute of being there. But that was summertime, boating time. It was shorts, flip-flops and swimming weather. We wondered what it would be like during other seasons, so Dani and I returned in September to celebrate our second wedding anniversary. This time it was just the two of us. We rented a dark, little log cabin type of house, with a private dock, and a boat. Sure enough the weather wasn't the same. It was rainy, a bit cold, and grey most of our stay. We still loved every second of it.

SPIRITUAL PLACES

Over the years, I have noticed there are certain places that touch my heart whenever I visit them, or even just think of them. New York City inspires me. The ocean resorts of Mexico and the Caribbean relax me.

I fell in love with Colorado, too. There was something spiritual about the place for me. The tree-covered mountains, the wildlife and wilderness, the spirit of the great outdoors seemed to become a part of me ever since that first week-long ski vacation in the winter of 2002.

Moving from Plano, Texas to Evergreen, Colorado was the first pure lifestyle move for me. It taught me how much living in a spiritual place improves my quality of life. Moving from Evergreen, Colorado to Camp Verde, Arizona was my second lifestyle move. There I had fallen in love with a redhead. I captured the spirit of that move in a poem I wrote to Dani on March 30, 2009 simply called, My Favorite Place:

> We met online and spoke of vacations far away...
> Brazil and Italy would be dream destinations to play...
>
> We imagined walking hand in hand...
> And lying together in the sand...
> We met the first time at a resort in Sedona...
> It was the first I laid eyes on Dani's Arizona...
>
> I got to know you beyond the net...
> I left feeling so happy that we'd met...
>
> You came to see me in the Evergreen trees...
> It was wonderful to have you here with me...

We called it 'Cook & Bake' and wow, did we
have fun...
I never knew how much I could enjoy
someone...

I acquired a large debt from your critique of
10+2 Readiness...
So I traveled to Camp Verde for the weekend
we dubbed 'Endless'...

We kissed, we hugged, and we loved each
other completely...
You marked my debt 'Paid in Full, absolutely
and unequivocally'...

We then met in the beautiful town of Newport
Beach...
For forty-eight hours you were within my
arm's reach...

We sang, we swam, and made plans for a new
King...
We shared incredible emotions that only true
love can bring...

A card you sent me should have given me the
clue...
What I have learned is something you already
knew...

"I've just discovered the most romantic little spot"... It read...
"It's in your arms"... What more needed to be said...?

We've talked of Hawaii, Quebec, or a quiet place on a lake...
Mexico, Italy, anywhere we can be together, for goodness sake...

A remote island, a busy city, it doesn't matter to me...
As long as I am with you then I am where I want to be...

It doesn't matter where we go... It doesn't matter what we do...
What I have come to understand... My favorite place to be is with you...

So my beautiful Dani... The places we visit will hold special charms...
But the magic of our love is being in one another's arms...

Sedona, Arizona became a "magical" spot for us. It was in Sedona, during our first weekend together that a stranger was so struck by our love she asked if she could take a picture of us. It's where we held the "best party ever" for our rehearsal dinner. We were married there on the grounds of our favorite resort, the

L'auberge De Sedona. We celebrated a lot of life and love in Sedona surrounded by the breathtaking natural beauty of its red rocks.

My third lifestyle move was made together with Dani. Lake living had touched something deep within us both. The water, the trees and the natural beauty had captured us. We have a feeling of peace and calm when we are there. It turns out my poem had been prescient. Two years after our rental try outs we found "our quiet place on a lake".

DREAM HOME

It was a short drive from the Charlotte International Airport to Lake Norman. It was late afternoon on a warm summer evening. There was very little traffic. And it was beautiful. Coming from the high, dry, hot plains of Northern Arizona, the lusciousness and greenness of the trees was incredible. It felt like we were driving on roads cut through a rain forest.

> *Lightning Bolt:* Suddenly, about twenty-five minutes into our drive, we saw the water. Driving over the first highway bridge of many, the water of Lake Norman surrounded us. We could see lake houses, private and public docks, restaurants, and boats… lots of boats. It was awesome.

Our realtor, Geena Witt, met us in the parking lot of a strip mall. For nearly a year, she and Dani had been previewing lake homes in North and South Carolina. Geena would see a new listing show up on the multiple listing service (MLS) realtors use and would screen it against Dani's list of requirements. If it fit the list, she would often go and take a look before sending it to Dani. They had previewed hundreds of homes before narrowing in down to the eight we'd be walking through.

The search focused on homes on Lake Norman and Lake Wiley. Both are man-made fresh water lakes fed by the Catawba River. They both had a history of maintaining useable water levels all year round. And they are both comfortable swimming temperature for much of the year. This was important because an accessible and useable lake was high on our list.

Lake Norman is located in North Carolina and is the larger of the two. It has 520 miles of shoreline and a surface area of more than 50 square miles. It touches eleven different cities north of Charlotte.

Lake Wiley straddles North and South Carolina. It has 325 miles of shoreline and a surface area of 21 square miles. Its settlements include Charlotte and four other cities to the south.
We saw four homes on Wednesday and four more on Thursday. On Friday, we went back to our favorites... one on Lake Wiley and the other on Lake Norman. It

was a tough decision because the Lake Wiley house was move-in ready, but the lakefront and property wasn't as nice as the Lake Norman house.

We choose the Lake Norman home based on schools, the location in the town of Mooresville, and the gorgeous property. Its long driveway winds down to a private lakefront retreat. The house is nestled on a picturesque waterfront lot, just under two acres. It has just over two hundred trees, and 454 feet of shoreline. The lake can be seen from nearly every window in the house with a spectacular 180-degree water view. It's almost impossible to see a road.

Another important determining factor was our discomfort with ostentatiousness, or to use the slang term, "bling". The Lake Wiley home looked like a mansion or a palace. It seemed to scream, "Look at me... I'm rich!" (Remember one of my life lessons from the last chapter, to live life without "arrogance".) The Lake Norman property was nice but comfortable. It said, "Come on in, join me on the back porch, have a cool drink and enjoy the beauty of the lake."

> *Lightning Bolt:* We both agreed that the Lake Norman house was the place we could live for the rest of our lives. The property was amazing. The house was comfortable and had enough plus points to work with. It was a good size and shape. It was situated well on the

property. All the things we didn't love about it could be fixed.

We flew back to Arizona on Saturday morning, October 19, 2013. Before leaving we made an offer to buy the Lake Norman house. When we landed in Phoenix, I turned on my cell phone and we learned the owner wanted more money than we had offered. By the time we made the eighty-mile drive home, we had negotiated the final price and an agreement was reached. The next day, we were under contract. We closed on the house two months later.

And so it was - Dani and I had bought our quiet place on a lake.

We had found the property of our dreams but the house didn't quite match up, not yet anyway. We embarked on what would become a furious seventeen-month remodeling project. It touched nearly every room in the house and the dock. It added four new rooms and a lakeside deck and storage area.

Our goal was to re-shape the house to fit dual purposes. First, we wanted a comfortable home in which to raise our children, and for Dani and me to live in for the rest of our lives. Second, we want it to be a destination place where we celebrate life and love with our family and friends.

After seventeen months of nearly non-stop construction, we have re-shaped the house into the home we want to live in, love in, play in, and entertain in for the rest of our lives.

LAKE TOYS

High on the list of the many wonderful attributes of lake living is play. I have to admit that we approached the accumulation of lake toys with urgency! When we moved to the lake, Dani and the girls traveled by air. They arrived on Friday, four days before me. That meant my wife had "free" time to shop for toys. And she went big.

On Monday evening, I drove into our rental home on Lake Norman. We had leased it for two weeks because the kitchen in our new home was being remodeled and we were waiting for the moving van to arrive. That evening we had dinner and celebrated the sale of the trade company. It was our first time together since the final closing of the deal.
The next morning, Dani drove me to a boat showroom. She had spent enough time there gathering information to narrow down the decision-making process for me. The latest models of pontoon boats were actually tri-toons, with three pontoons. Adding the third pontoon gives the boat more than enough speed for water skiing. So, she had determined a Bennington Tri-toon was the perfect solution for our first lake toy. She had made the

Matt Gersper

choice simple for me. I could choose the expensive one or the really expensive one, whichever I preferred.

I selected the expensive one because it came with an outboard motor meaning we wouldn't need to winterize it. And that meant we could use it all year long.

We bought our boat that very day and drove it home as a family, docking it in front of our temporary rental home on the lake. What a wonderful feeling. That boat was so much more than a boat – it was a symbol of transition for me on three levels:

- From an Arizonan to a North Carolinian.

- From a land-dweller to a lake-dweller.

- From the complex business of international trade to the fascinating business of Happy Living.

In fact, we named our boat Happy Living. The boat dealer installed our company logo on the boat when we took it in for the first service.

A few weeks later, we were on the hunt for jet skis. During Dani's research, we learned that "jet skis" were now called "personal water craft" (PWC), and that they had grown from relatively small and unstable

225

motor powered skis to very stable, very big and heavy, water motorcycles. We settled on a couple of brand new Yamaha PWC's. Dani got a beautiful, black 2014 FX Cruiser SHO that can flat out fly. She's taken hers over seventy miles per hour. Mine is the 2013 version of the same model. Not quite as fast but I am comforted by the fact that I get better gas mileage than her!

A few weeks later, we sent the girls off to summer camp. Dani and I had the house to ourselves for two weeks. We decided to try out paddle boarding. I had become interested in it after reading Laird Hamilton's book, Force of Nature[71]. I had tried it once before in Hawaii but had not been very successful. This time, Dani and I decided to rent boards for a week to see if we liked it. The rental company delivered them right to our home and gave us a fifteen-minute lesson on how to paddle. We also watched a few online instructional videos to learn, or at least see, proper technique.

In no time at all, we were paddling pretty comfortably around the lake, and having fun. In fact, we were enjoying it so much that we bought our own boards and paddles before the rentals had come due. We've since added another four inflatable paddleboards to our "fleet" so we can have fun exploring the lake with family and friends.

Our stable of lake toys is rounded out with a couple of towable tubes for pulling adventures behind the boat or jet skis, adult and child water skis, an assortment of inflatable "floaties" for lake lounging, a big floatable island that the girls love to play on, and a diving board we had installed on our dock. By our second summer on the lake, we were fully equipped. From here on out, the focus is officially shifted from buying lake toys to playing with lake toys.

ALL THINGS WATER

For the first half of my life I was a land-dweller who was drawn to the water. One of my major goals for the rest of my life is to become a lake-dweller developing mastery of all things water.

In an earlier chapter, I shared how I terrified my daughter crashing my jet ski over rocks at the lake edge and halfway up the rock wall that lines our property. Well, in my first year as a boat captain I also crashed our boat into a restaurant.

The lake has a few restaurants that we can boat to. During our first summer, we took the boat on a long trip to one of the lakeside restaurants three towns away. By car, it takes twenty minutes. By boat, it is about an hour.

Dani was captaining the boat on the way there. Upon arrival, the "easy to park" slips were all taken, so she had to carefully navigate around all the other boats to the last slip available. We docked the boat without incident and went in for lunch feeling pretty good about our boating skills.

However... we boarded our boat after lunch and discovered the boat parked next to us had left and been replaced by another much larger boat. This one was so long that it stuck out well beyond the length of the slip. I had already been worried about getting our boat out of the tight space it was in. Now it was even worse. I had to gently back up, then turn sharp right with very little clearance available between the front of our boat and the back of the long one next to us. The margin for error was very, very small. Somewhere during the backing and the turning and the worrying, I hit the gas when I shouldn't have and slammed the back of our boat into the side of the restaurant. It crashed so hard the patrons let out a collective gasp, my wife and daughters were nearly knocked off their feet from the jolt, and I got to experience feeling both stupid and embarrassed at once. People came running over from the restaurant to see what had happened.

It didn't take them long to figure it out. What they all saw, I'm sure, was a wannabe lake man captaining a brand new, fancy boat without having the slightest clue of what he was doing. Rather than mock me (and I wouldn't have blamed them if they had!), they helped me navigate out of the tight spot I was in. And they taught me a lesson.

The lesson was that boats on water do not behave like cars on land. Gravity and brakes give a driver decisive control of a car. Boats don't come with brakes. The water often plays an active role in moving a boat. I should have slowed down and asked for help instead of trying to drive the boat like a car.

Now I know to utilize others on board. I should have asked Dani to stand at the back of the boat and help me gently snuggle up close to the restaurant wall. I should have put Shea in the front of the boat as a look-out to make sure we cleared the back of the long boat. Most importantly, I should have relied more on "hands-on" maneuvering of our boat rather than powering and steering like a car.

While I have been spiritually drawn to the water, it's clear I do not possess a natural affinity for "all things water" in a practical sense. Mastering the water lifestyle is going to take time, lots of patience, and practice, practice, practice.

That's why I have dedicated the rest of my life to becoming a lake-dweller. I try to incorporate the water in as many parts of my daily life as possible. I make it a part of my exercise, meditation, entertainment, barbequing, and boating. I love jet skiing to a working breakfast, with my calendar, computer, and briefcase kept nice and dry in its large storage trunk. And my summer office (the end of our back-porch) has a beautiful view of the lake.

Given enough practice, with a commitment to learning new skills, and with enough time, I'm sure that even *I* can become a master of all things water.

We found the final piece to my water-based lifestyle in February 2015. Dani had been secretly looking for a new addition to our family. On a Monday morning, she casually asked me if I'd like to go buy a puppy. That afternoon we returned home with a beautiful half Britney Spaniel, half Blue Heeler mix. We named him Sir Charles Barkley because of the way he defended himself from the fierce claws of our three angry cats using his substantial backside as a shield.

Barkley, as we call him, shares my dedication to mastering all things water. He rides along on the boat, the jet skis, paddleboards, and he's even tackled towable tube riding. He loves to swim in the lake, and he's constantly by my side when my summer office is open. He also enthusiastically accepts his responsibility for goose patrol. He not only runs the geese off our property, but he even takes to the water to swim them off too! I sense that this lake man in the making has a canine partner with a similar mission!

So, here are my three key questions, the results they yielded and the lessons I learnt:

> WHAT?: To become a Master of All Things Water.

WHY?: Being close to the water gives me a feeling of peace and joy, and brings me closer to my soul.

HOW?: 10,000 hours of learning, practicing, and playing on, in, and around the lake.

Result: A lifetime of practice is in progress...

Who I am becoming: A lake-dweller incorporating the water in as many parts of my daily life as possible: exercising, meditating, entertaining, barbequing, boating, reading, writing, thinking, and playing.

MBG Life Lesson: Living in a spiritual place improves quality of life.

MBG Life Lesson: Find the place you want to live the rest of your life.

MBG Life Lesson: Invest in your house to make it your dream home.

MBG Life Lesson: People will become 'masters' at complex things when they have accrued 10,000-hours of practice.

Chapter 13 – Author
(2015...)

"Allow whatever you feel deep within you in that
quiet and peaceful space to guide you in the direction
that is your true destiny."
(Dr. Wayne W. Dyer)

As I have stated before, I believe every human being
has access to three astonishing powers to create their
absolute best life - powers which are often left
untapped. All three were at play as I transformed into
an author and motivational speaker. Happy Living was
up and running, and my mission to become a lake man
had begun in earnest. Now that I was firmly on my
path, the transformations were coming fast and
furious!

My recent transformations are also overlapping and
interweaving. My connection with nature and the lake
is fundamental to my experience of the Tao, which
helps me to grow and change as an author. While my
one true love infuses my entire life with the power of
love, which is fundamental to my work at Happy Living
and my understanding of the Tao and so on, with each
transformation informing the other.

My transformation into an author started in the spring
of 2015 with a series of coincidences, chance
meetings, and opportunities I could never have

dreamed of, let alone planned for. A progression of serendipitous happenings revealed to me a common human challenge – missing or not acting on the big inspirations of life. With it came a surprisingly simple solution – paying attention to *what* inspires you, understanding *why* it inspires you, and knowing *how* you'll bring it into your life. This dynamic combination of clear "problem" and obvious "solution" ignited in me the passion and the power to write a book. My clear sense of what truly matters to me, combined with my heart and the Universe itself (the 3 Powers activated) conspired to launch my career as a published author.

It all began at the world's largest Paleo event, called Paleo f(x), in Austin, Texas in the summer of 2015. My daughter and I attended the conference to learn about the Paleo lifestyle, and write about it for HappyLiving.com. During the conference we met Keith and Michelle Norris, the founders of Paleo f(x, and Seth Blaustein, who is the cofounder of another conference called Voice & Exit. Seth and I talked several times over the course of the weekend. I explained our work at Happy Living, and he explained that Voice & Exit is an annual conference exploring the future of technology, society and culture. We decided there may be an opportunity to collaborate and agreed to stay in touch.

In my days as the owner of the trade company I attended three or four conferences a year. It had long been my observation at conferences and other gatherings of like-minded people that it's very easy to get everyone inspired about something new in the moment, but much harder to get them to follow up afterwards. As an exhibitor at many conferences, it was always a simple task to get potential customers excited about a new service when I spoke to them. However, I found it extremely frustrating when they failed to take follow-up action upon returning home.

I decided to write a blog post about that. As a follow up to the Paleo event, I wrote *How to Maximize the Benefits of Any Conference*[72]. That post was the first small inspiration for what eventually became the book you are reading right now. The idea of *Turning Inspiration into Action* was born.

DAD, THIS IS YOUR BOOK

A short while after Paleo f(x), Seth Blaustein of Voice & Exit was preparing for his annual conference. As it turns out, they planned to introduce a new format on the second day that created an opportunity for me. This was called Harvest Squares, and the idea was to split the attendees into four groups and have them move from one workshop to the next over the period of four hours. He asked if I would take part in Harvest Squares as a speaker, conducting a workshop called *How to make the most of your V&E high*. He wanted me to help his attendees maximize the benefits of his conference, the very thing I had just written about, and of course I eagerly accepted.

Another opportunity presented itself by chance when one of the speakers was late. The conference organizers asked if, rather than working with the four smaller groups, I would conduct my workshop for all the delegates at once. I agreed, and soon all eyes were on me.

I had prepared a ten-minute TED Talk-style presentation to introduce myself, in which I shared the simple Process that I use to make big transformations in my life. I showed the audience how I applied the process to athletics, to business, to family life, to spiritual life, and even to my love life! Then I led the workshop, showing the delegates how they could apply the same process to turn inspirations discovered at the conference into action upon returning home.

It was great. The audience was engaged and I was in that state of flow where time disappears and communication is effortless. Everything felt right.

> *Lightning Bolt:* I felt different, in an amazing way, than during any other speaking engagement in my career. I could feel inspiration striking me like a lightning bolt.

My daughter Kaileen got a lightning bolt of inspiration, too. Walking back to the hotel, she said, "Dad, this is your book!"

CONNECTIONS AND KEYNOTES

The Voice and Exit conference was my second visit to Austin in as many months. I used the opportunity to follow up with some people Kaileen and I had met at the Paleo event. One of those meetings was a dinner with Keith and Michelle Norris. We had a wonderful time, enjoying great conversation and good food. That's when I learned about the swap arrangement between Paleo f(x) and Voice & Exit. Each conference invited the other to be their guest. Without this serendipitous swap, I would never have met Seth Blaustein or even known about Voice & Exit.

At dinner, Keith and Michelle talked about expanding their conference internationally. During my ten years in the trade business, I had developed a close relationship with Ann Lister, the cofounder of the International Compliance Professionals Association (IPCA). Ann and her organization have done a great job expanding internationally, so I asked Keith and Michelle if they would like me to introduce them to her. They said yes.

In the Austin airport, preparing for my flight home, I called and asked Ann's permission to introduce her to the Norris'. She agreed and then asked what I was doing in Austin. I told her about my workshop, how excited I was about it, and how Kaileen said that this should be the material for my first book. Ann replied, "You should do that at our conference."

The *Turning Inspiration into Action* keynote presentation was coming to life.

> *MBG Life Lesson*: Look for opportunities to help others by connecting them to people, products or services that can solve their problems, even when, or perhaps especially when, your doing so isn't self-serving.

I was excited. The very idea of helping others turn inspiration into action resonated deep within me.

In my life, I have discovered that coincidences, chance meetings and opportunities are often disguised as misfortune, too. What happened next was one of those disguised opportunities. At Happy Living, we had been preparing to host a retreat in Sedona, Arizona to teach the principles of our Seven Foundations of Health[73]. Our co-host was my friend and owner of KC's Family Tae Kwan Do, Karen Conover. As the deadline was approaching, we hadn't sold enough seats to make the event work. Rather than cancel it entirely, we moved it from an expensive resort to Karen's studio, shortened the format, and changed the focus to Turning Inspiration into Action. Suddenly, my keynote presentation had two gigs.

Delivering my message to the Tae Kwan Do students was exhilarating. I was more excited than ever about *Turning Inspiration into Action*.

AMAZON AGAIN

Full of ideas, enthusiasm, and some apprehension, I began doing research on how to write and publish my book. I quickly came across a book that sounded just right for me called *Book Launch: How to Write, Market & Publish Your First Bestseller in Three Months or Less AND Use it to Start and Grow a Six Figure Business*, by Chandler Bolt and James Roper.

I read this book in one weekend. For you, that may not sound impressive. For me, it's very, very unusual to read a book so fast. But I was excited to get going and I knew I had to complete this book before starting my new writing project.

I found the book interesting in these three ways:

Number one, it presented a simple, direct process called mind mapping[74] to organize my thoughts on paper before beginning the actual writing. It was a perfect fit for my logical, organized style of thinking.

Number two, the book presented industry-changing technology that resonated with me. In my two previous careers, I had been involved in decentralizing highly technical processes by creating software that could be used by frontline workers to produce faster, better, less expensive solutions. In their book, Chandler Bolt and James Roper taught me about the sophisticated tools available through Kindle Direct Publishing - tools which provide a regular person like me with the means to publish a book.

Number three, during my career in international trade, Amazon was the company that had breathed life into our young start-up business. After many months of negotiations, we had landed a large, multi-year project with them that gave us the resources and credibility to become a viable company. I thought, wouldn't it be interesting if Amazon is also the catalyst for launching my writing and speaking business.

It seemed as if the stars were aligning for me. All of this happened in the space of three months. During that time, there were three very different but equally powerful forces helping me along.

THE THREE POWERS: PRIORITY, HEART, AND UNIVERSE

Let's go back and review what had happened so far on my journey to becoming an author.

A speaking engagement touched me deeply and inspired me. It struck me as something important - but why?

When I thought about it, writing this book was a perfect fit for my life's mission to improve the health and wellbeing of the world, one person at a time. It provided me another way to give back some of what I have been given. It touched my heart's desire to help others.

It also fit my business strategy at Happy Living, particularly with a specific business objective to grow our speaking engagements. We are focused on the 3 C's: creating *content that inspires* through writing, building our *community*, and making *connections* with like-minded people and businesses. This book helps with each one.

It also perfectly fits my philosophy for lifelong work[75]:

- Writing is work I want to do for the rest of my life.

- It can be broadcast to the world, without any geographical limitations.

- It has near-zero marginal cost revenue. This means creating a product or a service once, and selling it over and over again.

Publishing this book in ebook form also aligns with a personal goal to digitize everything I can. Digital technology is changing how we live, work, and communicate. I am determined to digitize as many ideas, information, products, and services that help me live a happy and healthy life as possible, so that I may easily share them with others.

As I went through a process of asking why writing a book was important to me, the idea of it morphed into a new lifelong commitment to being an author.

Writing a book passed my filters test with flying colors, giving it the *Power of Priority*. Becoming an author touched on my heartstrings, my business-strings, my financial-strings, even my personal-strings.

Writing a book that can help people turn their inspirations into action touched the very core of who I am and that gave it the *Power of the Heart*.

The third power at play is *Power of the Universe*. I'd like to explore this Power for a moment by sharing one of my favorite quotes of all time.

> "Until one is committed, there is hesitancy, the chance to draw back, always ineffectiveness. Concerning all acts of initiative (and creation), there is one elementary truth that ignorance of which kills countless ideas and splendid plans: that the moment one definitely commits oneself, then Providence moves too. All sorts of things occur to help one that would never otherwise have occurred. A whole stream of events issues from the decision, raising in one's favor all manner of unforeseen incidents and meetings and material assistance, which

no man could have dreamed would have come his way. Whatever you can do, or dream you can do, begin it. Boldness has genius, power, and magic in it. Begin it now."[76]
— William Hutchison Murray

When I decided to write *How to Maximize the Benefits of Any Conference* an idea was born. When I spoke at the V&E conference, I was struck by a powerful feeling that somehow "turning inspiration into action" was important. It passed my filters, activating the Power of Priority. As I explored *why* it was important to me, I infused the idea with Power of the Heart because it resonated deep within my inner spirit. Then it seemed to take on a life of its own, as by beginning to take action, I had activated the Power of the Universe.

So, with the 3 Powers fully activated and working for me, seemingly unrelated events and connections began rising in my favor ("all manner of unforeseen incidents and meetings and material assistance", to quote Murray) which I never could have dreamed of. These combined to bring to reality the book you are looking at right now.

I wrote this book, dear Reader, to share intimate details of how the 3 Powers: the Power of Priority, the Power of the Heart and Power of the Universe, have worked in my life. It is my sincere wish that through sharing my experience of them, you will learn how to bring them into your life, too.

To recap, my Process for transformation requires that you answer three questions. These are:

    1. WHAT inspires you?

    2. WHY it is important to you?
    and

    3. HOW will you bring it into your life?

So, in relation to my transformation into an author, here are those three key questions with their answers.

    WHAT?: Writing a book to help others turn inspiration into action.

    WHY?: It touched on my heartstrings, my business-strings, my financial-strings, even my personal-strings.

    HOW?: I prioritize writing and learning about publishing, and I have made a lifelong commitment to the path of the author.

    Result: A lifetime of practice is in progress...

    Who I am becoming: An author.

Chapter 14 - Viking Funeral

"As a well-spent day brings happy sleep, so a life well
used brings happy death."
(Leonardo da Vinci)

It is July 4, 2064. That's right, 2064. My body has been
wrapped in cloth and laid to rest in a simple open
wooden box. Family and friends have gathered at our
lake home for my final farewell.

Just one month earlier, many of the same people had
joined me in celebrating my one hundred and third
birthday, on June 4, 2064 (six-four, sixty-four). After
one hundred and three years and thirty days, my
party in this world is over. It had been a full, fun,
adventurous life.

During the first half of my life I was a land-dweller
focused on football, raising a family and building
businesses.

I lived my second half at a quiet place on a lake with
my one true love, having successfully launched our
adorable daughters into the world, and enjoyed the
balanced, harmonious and organic growth of Happy
Living.

It was from that peaceful lakeside place that I spent
my last 50 years immersed in mastering the things I

244

loved most. It had taken me forty-six and a half years to find my soul mate, my best friend, my beautiful Dani. I was so very fortunate to be able to love her for more than fifty-six years. The adventures we had, the memories we made, and the love we shared with family and friends will live on well beyond my passing.

It had taken me fifty years to discover the Tao Te Ching. It's ironic that Bob Buford (author of *Halftime*) asks his readers to choose the *one big thing* that's the most important to their life. The way he actually says it is, 'What's in your box?' I put the Tao in my box because it was my path to becoming all I am capable of being. After fifty-three years of study, I lay in a box peacefully as a simple man of the Tao. It is the very essence of the Tao to live as an example that may help others make choices aligned to their true selves. If my life has helped even one person make right choices for themselves, the joy that brings to the world will live well beyond my passing.

It had taken me nearly fifty-three years before I introduced Happy Living to the world. For the last fifty years I dedicated my professional time and resources to researching and experimenting with concepts, products, and resources that promote health and happiness.

Our mission at Happy Living for the past fifty years has been to improve the health and wellbeing of the world, one person at a time. One great thing about a business is it can live on well beyond the passing of its founder, and our mission will continue long into the future. If Happy Living helps even one person after my passing, it will be a wonderful testament to our great system of capitalism and free enterprise.

It took the first half of my life, more than fifty-four years, before I discovered my calling to write books, too. Sitting in my summer office, overlooking our lake, I made a lifelong commitment to transform myself into an author.

I remember the passing of my Tao mentor Dr. Wayne W. Dyer on August 29, 2015. I continued reading his words of wisdom for nearly fifty years after he died, all the way up to my peaceful passing in 2064. If the lessons in my books can help even one person after I have completed this physical life, it will give meaning to every hour I spent writing these past forty-eight years.

It took the first half of my life to reach our quiet place on a lake. For the second fifty years, I have incorporated the water in as many parts of my daily life as possible. In my five decades as a lake-dweller, I have practiced, learned new skills, and dedicated lots of time to develop mastery of all things water.

Of course, that doesn't make me a Viking King but a lake burial seems befitting for a Master of All Things Water.

So... with family and friends gathered around our lakeside patio, the pallbearers hoist the wooden box on my 11' 10" long, Amundson Hawaii paddleboard, walk me carefully down the wide staircase of our lakeside patio, and lay me gently on the water. One by one, the guests approach to pay their last respects and lay flowers on my body.

Finally, the love of my life comes to my side. Her beauty and grace defy her ninety years. She pauses for a moment, taking in the finality of it all, and leans in close to me for one last kiss.

The pallbearers hold their torches to the wooden box until the flames are strong. Then, with one powerful thrust in unison, they send me out onto the lake beneath a sky full of holiday fireworks. It is a glorious farewell to my one true love, my family and friends, and the quiet place on the lake I have loved so much.

PART 3: Transforming You

As I write these words, it's the month of December, in the year 2015 not 2064. I am excited to close out one great year and open a brand new one.

I am looking forward to spending my time in the New Year working on my unfinished transformations. And I'll keep myself tuned for inspiration to strike by paying attention to WHAT I am attracted to. It's going to be a great year. My practice of continuous improvement has created a momentum in my life such that each and every year gets better. I can't wait to get started.

I want that excitement and eagerness to be present for you too! So, before we take that journey together, let's briefly remind ourselves of where we have been.

In Part 1, I introduced the transformational practice I use to create my absolute best life. I revealed my 3-step process of WHAT, WHY and HOW. This works for anyone desiring a better life, and it will work for you if you make the commitment to it. The Process unleashes three powers, the Power of Priority, the Power of the Heart and the Power of the Universe to overcome the forces of Gravity holding a life in place.

In Part 2, I shared intimate details of transformations in my life so you could see the Process in action. You may have noticed I've had plenty of ups and downs along the way. That's just how it goes. What matters is that you focus more on the ups, don't let the downs get you down, and keep moving forward on your journey.

My transformational practice keeps me working to progress in a purposeful direction with consistency. Consistently working to create a better me helps me endure tough times and overcome the forces of Gravity of my life. I have shared my stories of transformation here in the hope that they will inspire you to want to make your own transformations. Now we come to Part 3, which is all about transforming you.

Chapter 15 - First Steps

"You have brains in your head.
You have feet in your shoes.
You can steer yourself
Any direction you choose."
(Dr. Seuss)

Dear Reader, in my view, the way to a better life is through creating a better you.

It's not about events, or circumstances, or luck, or conditions. It doesn't come from "out there". It's not given to you by your parents, or your boss, or your spouse, or your government.

It comes from inside you. It comes from "in here". This is good news because it means you are completely in charge. Creating a better you is all about recognizing and cultivating your inner self. Your absolute best life comes from taking personal responsibility to realize your full potential as a human being. Deciding to create a better you is a personal decision. And it's a decision you can make today!

Say it out loud. Right now. Say, "*Deciding* to begin the journey to my absolute best life is my decision to make!"

Now, say it louder!

Great.

There are three steps you can take today that will *start* you on your journey. I promise if you do these three things, if you embrace them fully and commit to them completely, your life will take off in ways you cannot begin to imagine from where you stand right now.

Are you ready?

Your life is about to change.

STEP ONE: PERSONAL RESPONSIBILITY

Have you heard people say "My pants don't fit me anymore"? Have you said it yourself?

It's an all too common phrase in our modern language. It underscores a dangerous shift from a culture of personal responsibility to one of blaming others. If I say, "I don't fit into my pants anymore" then I'm responsible. Yet somehow it's easier for me to blame my pants, as if they did the changing.

The first step to a better you is accepting personal responsibility for developing your full potential as a human being.

This is completely within your control. It comes from inside you.

Say it out loud. "I accept *personal responsibility* to develop my full potential as a human being."

Now, find a pen and paper and write it down. Yep, right now.

Post it around the house. Put a reminder in your wallet or purse. Dedicate yourself to personal responsibility from today forward.

STEP TWO: KAIZEN

The second step is deciding to develop a practice of Kaizen, or continuous improvement. As you may remember from Chapter 2, as a personal practice, Kaizen is the idea that there is always something that you can do better tomorrow than you did today.

A practice dedicated to continuous improvement increases your commitment to a lifetime of learning and trying new things. What it is that you decide to improve upon at any given time can vary widely - it may be a craft, or an art, or a physical skill, or a spiritual practice. It could be expanding your capacity for kindness, or becoming a better listener, or tolerating others more graciously. It might be trying to sleep, or exercise, or eat, better. It can be big or small. It can be anything that you want to do better.

The decision is completely yours to make. It too comes from inside you.

252

Say it out loud. "I've decided to start a daily practice of *continuous improvement*."

Write it down.

Read about Kaizen. Make a list of things you want to improve. Start work on one of them today, even if it's just taking a single small step – looking something up online, for example. Dedicate yourself to the practice of Kaizen from this day forward.

And never look back, ever. Unless you are in immediate danger of crashing a boat into a restaurant, that is!

STEP THREE: CAREFREE DILIGENCE

The third step is deciding to begin a practice of carefree diligence.

In his book, *The Tao of Joy Every Day: 365 Days of Tao Living*[77], Derek Lin says that

Diligence means having the "discipline to progress in a purposeful direction with consistency". He continues: "It's taking one step after another, without stopping but also without a frantic rush. The body may be in motion, but the mind is perfectly relaxed" as you enjoy the journey to your absolute best life.

The key words here are *motion* and *relax*. It's important that you keep moving on your journey but

RELAX about it. Keep doing but stop stressing. Enjoy the process but don't cling to outcomes. Trust in yourself that every small effort is a step on your journey, regardless of the immediately observable result.

Once again, this decision is completely within your control.

Isn't that great?

You don't need permission from anyone. You can decide today. Right now.

Say it. Out loud. "I've decided to begin my practice of *carefree diligence*."

Write it down.

Put reminders everywhere. Make a deep commitment to yourself to begin the practice of carefree diligence, starting *now*.

How do you feel now? Energized? Eager for more? Great!

PRACTICE FOR LIFE

Once you've made the commitment to take personal responsibility for developing your full potential (step one), and started your journey using steps two

(Kaizen) and three (Carefree Diligence), don't be downhearted if things don't immediately improve. Mastering the practices of *kaizen* and *carefree diligence* will take time. That's why they're called practices. Think of it this way. It's taken you your entire life to get where you are today. What if it takes another 10,000 hours to master these practices? What if it takes the rest of your life? As Confucius said, "It does not matter how slowly you go, as long as you do not stop."

So go slowly. Be kind to yourself. But keep moving forward in a purposeful direction with consistency. Use Shunryu Suzuki-roshi's message to be gentle and resolved at the same time. Remind yourself that you are perfect just the way you are, and yet keep looking for ways to make a little improvement.

Take your time. Do your work. And learn as you take daily steps on the journey to your absolute best life.

> *MBG Life Lesson:* Keep doing but stop stressing.

You're in charge now. In fact, you're in charge from here on out. If your pants don't fit, it's your responsibility to change yourself back to the size you were when they did. Or buy some new ones. If your life doesn't fit the way you want it to, it's up to you to transform it by transforming you. When you accept personal responsibility, you can steer yourself in any direction you choose.

Chapter 16 - Inspiration

"Life isn't about finding yourself. Life is about creating
yourself."
(George Bernard Shaw)

Congratulations.

You have decided to begin the journey to your
absolute best life. Where do you want to go? What do
you want to do? Who do you want to become?

Wait. Stop!

I don't want you to answer those questions. I want
you to *ask* them.

Ask yourself, "Where would I go if I could go
anywhere?"

Wonder aloud, "What would I do if I knew I would not
fail?"

Hold the thought, "Who do I want to become as I
begin the work of developing my full potential as a
human being?"

Then I want you to pay attention. Don't answer. Just
pay attention. Go about your work and live your life,

and pay attention to what comes to you. Begin your practices of *kaizen* and *carefree diligence* and notice the people, places and things that inspire you.

When you ask WHAT inspires you, you'll start seeing things differently and seeing different things.

You are brainstorming with your life. Do not filter things out, just yet. Do not ignore something that may appear far-fetched or crazy or unrealistic. Remember my seaplane? At the WHAT stage, I just felt excited when I saw it and thought it was cool. I didn't apply any filters to the idea of buying one until later in the Process. So, for now, just notice WHAT attracts your attention, with no judgment.

You are exploring what *you* want to do with the rest of your life. Not what your parents want you to do. Not what your boss thinks you should do. Not what your spouse, or family or friends, or culture expects you to do. Not even what *you* expect of yourself.

Give yourself this beautiful gift. Simply take some time and pay attention to what inspires you.

Don't rush. Enjoy. Keep asking the question WHAT? WHAT? WHAT? There's nothing for you to do except engage with the world around you. Watch for little things or great big ideas that grab your attention. Anything. Explore any opportunities or inspirations that you find attractive. If you feel an impulse to go to a new place, try a new class or call an old friend, act on it and then notice what grabs you while you have that experience. Treat it as an intriguing game. There is a never-ending stream of data and information flowing to you. Pay attention. Get curious. Discover *what* grabs you.

WHAT you find inspiring is very important. Remember, this is the first step to accessing enough personal power to overcome the Gravity holding you in place. It's tapping into the power you need to start moving your life forward.

Your work in this phase is to sift through the constant barrage of information available to you, searching for golden nuggets that will help you on your journey to your absolute best life. Asking WHAT you want and paying attention is how you prepare yourself so inspiration comes to you, like a bolt of lightning.

Oh, and this is really important... don't forget to have fun. Having fun is a very strong indicator that you're on the right track.

Take lots of notes, too, and find pictures that inspire you, whether you take photos, draw, or cut things out from magazines. Do whatever you need to do to keep track of your inspirations, and to stay connected to them.

Chapter 17 – Reflection

"Within, within, this is where the world's treasure has
always been."
(Lao Tzu[78])

Never forget that you are magnificence in human
form. There is infinite power hidden inside you. The
key to accessing that power is doing the things you
love; doing the things that are most important to you.
You tap into amazing power when you're doing things
that are deeply meaningful to you.

Your tool for this work is reflection.

Asking the question WHAT has helped you build a big
inventory of ideas, opportunities, and inspirations that
you find attractive. Keep doing that. Keep paying
attention to what grabs your attention. Keep building
your inventory from the ever-flowing stream of data
and information coming into your life.

Now you can start asking WHY, too. Asking WHY is the
process of choosing the things that touch your heart.
This is how you determine what is attractive to you
AND is in alignment with who you are – deep inside!

Look at the notes, or pictures, or lists you created to
keep track of your inspirations. Immerse yourself in
each item. Ask, "Is this really important to me?" If you

answer no, move on to the next item. Like with my seaplane. It was super cool but not really important to me. Let it go. Just say no and move on, no judgment.

If you answer yes to something, then ask yourself the next question, WHY?
Why is it important? Think deeply when answering. Take your time and reflect on your answers. Put them in one of two categories: The heart and the head.

Your head tells you all the things you "should" do. It is filled with advice and expectations from your parents, your boss, your spouse, your family and friends, and culture. All this energy comes from outside you. That makes it weak. None of it is strong enough to overpower Gravity. Head-based reasons do not create enough energy to overcome procrastination, blame, self-doubt, what others say and other forces of Gravity holding your life in place.

Your heart knows the things you want to do. When an inspiration touches your heart, it's a signal that that inspiration is aligned with your inner spirit. And how do you tell if something has touched your heart? By the way you feel, of course. You feel good. You may have to get still and quiet to feel those stirrings of excitement deep inside your chest, or you may be overpowered by a wave of thrill at your new idea and have to dance around the room. Or anywhere in between. But you'll be able to feel it. Heart-based reasons come from love (in here), not expectation (out there). Doing things based on love makes you very powerful. It's how I felt holding Kaileen in my arms for the first time. I could "feel" I was ready to transform into a provider. That's the power you get when you align what you do with who you are. Following your heart activates a great power within you.

My practice of reflection helped me create the Seven Wonders of My Life that I introduced in Part 1. To remind you, these are:

1. *My one true love*: being a loving and devoted husband.

2. *My family*: providing love, support, and leadership.

3. *My friends*: connecting and celebrating life together.

4. *Fitness*: caring for my body, mind, and spirit.

5. *Finance*: investing in charities, businesses, and people doing good work.

6. *Adventure*: exploring different places, new experiences, and fresh ideas.

7. *Business*: researching, experimenting, and writing about best practices for Happy Living.

These are my filters for deciding what is truly important to me, and what is not.

So, what have you discovered about yourself during this exercise of asking WHY? What are the "Wonders" of your life so far? What are your filters?

Reflection and filtering help you to build a prioritized life. That creates energy and power in two ways:

First, by eliminating things that are not important to you, you make space for those that are. The more you say "No" to what you don't want, the more time, energy and resources you will have for what matters most to you. Say no to everything you possibly can so you can spend more time on your yeses. This gives you the *Power of Priority*.

The second source of power comes from anchoring. Filtering helps you say, "This is in, and that is out." Anchoring answers the question of WHY something is so important to you. The love I felt holding Kaileen was deeply anchored to me. I would have done anything to give her everything she needed to become happy and successful in life. When you anchor your ideas, opportunities and inspirations to the wonders of your life, you ignite the *Power of the Heart*.

The pursuit of happiness is a never-ending journey. Remember the quote we examined earlier: "No man ever steps in the same river twice, for it's not the same river and he's not the same man." Who you are and what you want is constantly evolving. WHAT is possible for you today is very different from what *was* possible twenty years ago, and what *will be* possible twenty years from now. That's how life is. It is constantly changing and so are you.

You are perfect just as you are and you could use a little improvement.

Make a constant practice of paying attention to WHAT you are attracted to, and WHY. Doing so will keep you evolving in a positive direction, constantly advancing your life based on who you are and what you want.

Continuously creating a better you takes work. There are many forces trying to hold your life in place. Prioritizing your life around what's most important to you, and anchoring changes to who you are and what you want gives you power, energy, and will to overcome the forces of Gravity of your life.

Trust yourself. What you feel deep within you, in that quiet and peaceful space of reflection, will guide you on your journey to your absolute best life. Your heart knows where your happiness lies, so listen to it carefully.

Chapter 18 - Action

"The only thing that is constant is change."
(Heraclitus)

Let's look at what you've already accomplished.

1. You decided to create a better you.

2. You accepted personal responsibility to develop your full potential as a human being.

3. You decided to start a daily practice of continuous improvement.

4. You committed to beginning a practice of carefree diligence.

5. You started building an inventory of WHAT inspires you.

6. You created the Wonders of Your Life to use as filters for deciding WHY one thing is important to you, and another is not.

7. You anchored the changes you want in your life to something deeply important to

you (I'll call these *Your Changes* for the
remainder of the book).

8. You're developing an on-going practice of
    paying attention to WHAT inspires you
    and WHY.

That's a lot of work. I am proud of you. I hope you are
proud of you too.

Now it's time to change your life. Change starts by
making the firm commitment to transform yourself
from the person you are today, living the life you
currently have, into the person you want to be, living
the life of your dreams.

Are you ready?
In order to change your life, you must change who you
are and what you do. You must figure out HOW you
will bring change into your life.

In Part 1, I introduced the four areas on which to
concentrate when making big changes in your life:
time, routines, resources and focus. Now that I've
shared my own story with you, and you've had time to
reflect on your WHATs and WHYs, we will examine
them again in order to help you plan HOW you will
make your inspirations a reality.

TIME

You want more from your life. You have carefully selected Your Changes. You know these changes will improve your life. You weren't working on these changes yesterday. Tomorrow you will be. Therefore, today, your task is to work out how to make time for them.

The first thing to do is determine the specific actions you must take to bring each change into your life. And then determine how much time each action will take.

So now, make a list of everything you must do for Your Changes. Use the list as your guide. Check off items after completing them. Add to the list as you learn something new. Re-prioritize the order of the list as needed. Celebrate as you make progress. Each small step is taking you closer to the change you want to bring into your life.

With your action item list complete, it's time to decide how much time you will give to your change projects. Make your time commitment smaller than you want. If you think you can dedicate two hours a day, seven days a week, I would recommend changing it to ninety minutes a day, five days a week. Start smaller but be dedicated to your time commitment.
Consistently dedicating time may be the most important element of bringing change into your life.

Think about this for a minute. You have decided you want more from life. You built a big list of WHAT inspires you. You reflected on WHY one thing on the list is more important to you than another. You anchored specific changes to something deeply important to you. And you've decided to dedicate x minutes a day, y days a week to bring those changes into your life.

Make your time commitment something you know you can do. Then make it non-negotiable. Just show up and put in the time. Your absolute best life depends on it. Remember, it doesn't matter how slowly you go, so long as you do not stop.

Once you've decided how much time you'll be dedicating to bring Your Changes into your life, decide what you can give up. Make a list of how you spent your time the last month, or last year. Review the list in the same way that you reviewed the inventory of WHAT inspires you. Compare it to the Wonders of Your Life to filter out everything that's not *really* important to you. These are the things you can give up. You're wasting precious time on them. They are not bringing enough joy or value to your life.

Try to create at least as much time by giving up things as the time you've committed to Your Changes. I'd shoot for a little more. For example, if you've dedicated five hours a week for Your Changes, try to clear seven hours off your weekly calendar. Drop everything you can that is not important to you.

> *MBG Life Lesson:* If you want to bring changes into your life, you must make the space for them.

ROUTINES

As I wrote in Chapter 1, routines and habits are what keep a life in order. Remember, it takes twenty-one days to form a habit. The more you do something, the easier it gets to keep doing it. At some point, it becomes automatic.

If you are ready to bring Your Changes to life and transform yourself, you must re-order the routines in your life, and build new habits to support the change you are after. Write out your new schedule to prioritize time for Your Changes. Just looking at it will bring you joy because it reflects the person you intend to become. If it doesn't, this is a good time to find out, and you can go back to asking "What?" And "Why?" for a while longer.

RESOURCES

Time may be the most valuable resource for making change, but, as I wrote in Part 1, there are others, such as money, connections, libraries, schools, the Internet, service providers, and even social pressure.

Are there things for you to research? Are there books that will help you? Is there a school or a coach that would help you bring Your Changes into your life? What resources are at your disposal to support Your Changes? Think creatively here. Start with what you can. You can always add more as you go.

FOCUS

Remember, the firm decision to bring Your Changes into your life brings with it a change in focus. The actual decision itself will change how you see the world, and what you notice around you.

Once you made the decision to change your life, you started transforming you. With each item you check off your action list, you are evolving into a more fully realized person. As a more fully realized person, you see the world differently.
No man or woman ever steps in the same river twice, right?

Stay focused on the changes you're after. Keep evolving as a person. Continue your practice of paying attention to WHAT inspires you and WHY.

You'll soon see a brand new world.

TWO 'REALITY CHECKS' TO HELP GUIDE YOU

I mentioned earlier how my filters help me choose what is important to me and eliminate everything else. Filters help me say YES to ideas, opportunities and inspirations that are in alignment with my heart. They also help me to quickly say NO to everything else, which is just as vital. There are also two "reality checks" I use at the HOW stage which help me confirm that the change I am choosing truly fits who I am and what I want.

Reality Check 1: How are you spending your time after making the decision?

If you are struggling to find the time you need to make the change, then you may not have made the right choice. If it is difficult to decide what must be given up to make space, then your change may not be in full alignment with who you are. If making time for a new exciting inspirational idea is hard in the beginning, it is a signal that you don't have it right.

Alternatively, struggling to make time could also be a sign that you need to examine your core beliefs and align with those that truly serve you[79]. For example, a desire to start a new business may feel as if it is in conflict with being a good parent. This conflict may hold you in place and prevent you from moving forward with your idea. You may have to examine your belief that being a good parent means being

271

constantly available for your children. Perhaps it means showing them an example of someone who is happy and fulfilled by doing work which is meaningful to them, too. By re-examining your resources, you could take practical action to ease this conflict too, such as pausing work to be there for your children after school and then continuing after they are in bed, or having a rule that you will not work weekends.

If you discover you've made a choice that's not right for you, it's OK. Fail fast. Drop it and move on without judgment. You tried something that you thought would be good for you but discovered otherwise. No problem. Keep looking. Life is too precious and too short to waste time on wrong choices. And, of course, once you have decided to drop something, communicate your decision as clearly and kindly as you can to anyone else involved.

Reality Check 2: Can you see yourself going the distance?

The second reality check requires a bit of reflection and soul searching. In his book, *Outliers*[80], Malcolm Gladwell explains that people will become "masters" at complex things when they have accrued 10,000-hours of practice. Can you imagine spending 10,000 hours on your new exciting inspirational idea? Can you envision not only bringing it into your life, but also gaining mastery of it? If the answer is "no", let it go. Again, fail fast. Move on! If the answer is "YES", you've really found something special and life changing. That's how I felt about my decision to become an author. Could I imagine my sixty-year-old self, and my eighty-year-old self, and even my one-hundred-year-old self sitting on my porch, looking out over my lake, and writing my next book? Absolutely, unequivocally, YES!

WORK IS THE SIGNAL

I believe people are happiest when they are engaged in meaningful work. The work is where you find joy and contentment. Making the time. Doing the work. Focusing your attention on what you want. It is in *the doing* of things that are most important to you that you find true happiness.

More than that, the work signals to the Universe that you are all in! The moment you fully commit yourself and begin the work, you tap into the *Power of the Universe*. All sorts of things begin to happen to support you in your effort to make Your Changes. You ignite a whole stream of future connections, unforeseen incidents, meetings and assistance that you could never have imagined.

Be brave. Be bold. When Murray said, "Boldness has genius, power, and magic in it," he was talking to you.

BURN THE BOATS

Remember Confucius: "It does not matter how slowly you go as long as you do not stop."

That's the point. You use the Power of Priority to make a thoughtful decision to change something *very important* for your life, so you do not stop. There is no going back.

By anchoring Your Changes to what is truly important to you, deep within your spirit, you unleash the Power of the Heart. It'll provide the energy you need to overcome Gravity and sustain the change. When you decide, take action, get focused, get into it... when you "burn the boats" so you cannot return to your previous life, you evoke the Power of the Universe. Answering the three questions (WHAT, WHY, HOW) and committing to burning the boats will prepare you well to endure the long journey on the way to your absolute best life.

Change may be hard but you are ready. Change requires time, routines, resources and focus and you've made plans for these. Your Changes are deeply important to you, so you got this. You know how to connect to the powers you need to overcome any obstacle on the way to the life of your dreams.

You will not stop.

There is no going back.

Keep doing but stop stressing.

Chapter 19 - Patience

"Trust yourself. Create the kind of self that you will be
happy to live with all your life. Make the most of
yourself by fanning the tiny, inner sparks of possibility
into flames of achievement."
(Golda Meir)

How do you feel?

I hope you are inspired. I hope you can't wait to start
developing your full potential as a human being. I
want you to be excited about transforming you, and
creating your absolute best life.

I am excited for you.

Now I want you to start slowly. Be super kind to
yourself. Be patient. Focus on the work you love, not
the outcomes you want. Start small. Go slow. Go easy
but do not stop.

> *MBG Life Lesson:* The journey of a lifetime
> takes an entire lifetime.

It's taken your entire life to get to this point. It didn't
happen all at once, did it? Over all your years, it was
the accumulation of little actions, daily decisions, your
reactions to the events of life, and the passing of time
that led you right to where you are at this moment.

Now you've decided you want more. And you can have more. You can have everything you desire in life. That's what I believe. But you can't have it all tomorrow.

So take it easy. Here is my advice to help you enjoy the journey of the rest of your life.

- Make a firm commitment to a lifetime of *personal responsibility* and *continuous improvement*.

- Use *reflection* and develop a practice of paying attention to WHAT you are attracted to.

- Create filters for deciding WHY one thing is important to you, and another is not. This releases the *Power of Priority*.

- Anchor Your Changes to what is most important to you, the *Wonders of Your Life*. Doing so unleashes the *Power of the Heart*

- Prepare for HOW you'll bring change into your life, considering the time, new routines, and resources you'll need.

- Make lots of space for change by saying NO to things in your life that do not serve you.

- Take action, get focused, get totally into it, and *burn the boats*. Doing the work invokes the *Power of the Universe*.

- Practice *carefree diligence*. Keep doing but stop stressing. Enjoy the process but don't cling to outcomes.

Your heart knows where your happiness lies. Trust it. Trust yourself. Every day, every small effort is a step on the journey to your *absolute best life*.

Just keep stepping.

Enjoy it.

And be kind to yourself.

Wishing you a most magnificent life,

Matt Gersper

Final Thoughts

"Go confidently in the direction of your dreams. Live the life you have imagined."
(Henry David Thoreau)

Dear Reader, I want to thank you for sharing the journey of this book with me.

Before I go, I'd like to offer these final thoughts from some people whose words have made a difference in my life, and helped me on my journey.

> *From Sir Isaac Newton:* An object in motion will stay in motion... (Me: So get your life in motion!)

> *From Paulo Coelho, The Alchemist*[81]*:* When we strive to become better than we are, everything around us becomes better too.

> *From Paul Hawken*[82]*, author of Growing a Business:* Relax. Take your time. Work, practice and learn.

> *From Billy Joel*[83]*:* Slow down, you're doing fine. You can't be everything you wanna be before your time.

From me: Keep asking WHAT, WHY, and HOW… Keep searching for ways to improve yourself… every day, for the rest of your days… That's how you create the life of your dreams ☺

MBG Life Lessons: The Complete Collection (So Far!)

"The more I learn, the more I realize how much I
don't know."
(Albert Einstein)

Here is a summary of all the life lessons I have learnt
along my journey. I hope they may be of some value
to you on yours, and I wish you all the joy and peace
in the world as you walk your path and gather life
lessons of your own.

> Follow your heart wherever it leads you
> because it knows where your happiness lies.

> Efficiency is doing things right, effectiveness is
> doing the right things.

> All of you are perfect just as you are and you
> could use a little improvement.

> It does not matter how slowly you go as long
> as you do not stop.

> I can accomplish anything I set my mind to if I
> am willing to work long enough and hard
> enough for it.

I'd rather follow my own dreams and fail than conform to "what I am supposed to do" and succeed.

Your day belongs to another's dream.

When I have a problem, I take it to the top. When you want to lead change, clearly demonstrate the benefits of changing to others.

We have within us the power to control our minds or to be controlled by them.

My dreams are mine alone. I cannot presume that others think like me or want what I want.

Be bold and ask for what you want. Boldness has genius, power, and magic in it.

Take the risk, act when you're scared, it's unlikely that you'll be eaten today.

It's hard to distinguish between good luck and bad luck[84]. Many of the highest points in my life have led to low points, and visa versa.

It's better to ask for forgiveness than to ask for permission.

Relationships are as important as financial success to create an enduring business.

If a business idea isn't good enough to convince others to invest in it, it isn't good enough.

The way to market a service company is by its leaders becoming known as experts in their industry.

Collective intelligence is always greater than individual intelligence.

Be curious. Ask the next question.

You can't steer a Jet Ski without power, and you can't control the fate of a business without voting control.

Go deep into a specialty. Get a customer. Make them happy. Then repeat...

Find work you want to do for the rest of your life, with products and services that can be broadcast to the world, with highly recurring revenue, and near-zero marginal cost.

Pay attention to and act on what attracts you.

Soul Mates exist.

Drop the filters. Go big for what you truly want.

To touch someone's life is more valuable than any amount of money.

Don't resist life. Accept it as it is. It's the only way it can be.

Stress is caused by non-acceptance. Clinging to a notion that things *should be* different creates damaging stress in the body.

It's easier to maintain order than to correct disorder.

Live life without arrogance and without apology.

Develop a persistent willingness to say YES to opportunities for self-improvement.

Practice self-improvement as a way of life. Living in a spiritual place improves the quality of life.

Find the place you want to live for the rest of your life.

Invest in your house to make it your dream home.

People will become "masters" at complex things when they have accrued 10,000-hours of practice.

Look for opportunities to help others by connecting them to people, products or services that can solve their problems, even when, or perhaps especially when it isn't self-serving.

Keep doing but stop stressing.

If you want to bring changes into your life, you must make the space for them.

The journey of a lifetime takes an entire lifetime.

References:

1: Happyliving.com: "How to Maximize the Benefits of Any Conference". Web. <http://www.happyliving.com/?s=How+to+Maximize+the+Benefits+of+Any+Conference>

2: Happyliving.com: "Voice & Exit: a Festival Focused on Flourishing". Web. <http://www.happyliving.com/2015/06/17/voice-and-exit/>

3: Physicsclassroom.com: "Newton's Laws - Lesson 1 - Newton's First Law of Motion". Web. <http://www.physicsclassroom.com/Class/newtlaws/u2l1d.cfm#balanced>

4: Happyliving.com: "The Best Way to Overcome Judgment". Web. <http://www.happyliving.com/2014/07/02/overcome-judgment/>

5: "Empowering Inspiring video message." YouTube. November 23 2007. Web. <https://www.youtube.com/watch?v=D4zWBHFCmXM&feature=related>

6: Ted.com: "Viktor Frankl: Why Believe in Others". Web. <https://www.ted.com/talks/viktor_frankl_youth_in_search_of_meaning>

7: Frankl, Viktor E. Man's Search for Meaning. Beacon Press, 2006. Print.

8: Happyliving.com: "Live Like Nothing is Missing". Web.

<http://www.happyliving.com/2015/07/15/live-like-nothing-is-missing/#fn-2756-1>
9: "Never Say Can't- Jennifer Bricker." YouTube. September 1 2014. Web.
<https://www.youtube.com/watch?v=ho9M6r5RF4A&feature=youtu.be>
10. Home-school.com: "Soul Survivor: The Bethany Hamilton Story". Web.
<http://www.home-school.com/Articles/soul-surfer.php>
11: "Bethany Hamilton | How Does She Do It | One Arm Surf Girl" YouTube. April 10 2014. Web.
<https://www.youtube.com/watch?v=FX8tW5z_aik>
12: Wikipedia.com: "Fred Biletnikoff". Web.
<https://en.wikipedia.org/wiki/Fred_Biletnikoff>
13: Gersper, Matt and Sues, Kaileen. *The Belief Road Map*. Happy Living Books Independent Publishing, 2016. Print.
14: Wikipedia.com: "Shunryu Suzuki". Web.
<https://en.wikipedia.org/wiki/Shunry%C5%AB_Suzuki>

15: Burningboats.com: "A Historical Excursus". Web.
<http://burningboats.com/about-burningboatscom/>
16: Self-publishingschool.com: "About Self-Publishing School". Web. <http://self-publishingschool.com/about-sps/>
17: Wikipedia.com: "Quonset Hut". Web.
<https://en.wikipedia.org/wiki/Quonset_hut>

18: Profootballhof.com: "(Not So) Fast Freddy". Web. <http://www.profootballhof.com/news/not-so-fast-freddy/>

19: Wikipedia.com: "Wayne Dyer". Web. <https://en.wikipedia.org/wiki/Wayne_Dyer>

20: Happyliving.com: "Something Significant: One Simple Thing – The Legacy of U.C. Davis Football". Web. <http://www.happyliving.com/2015/02/04/something-significant-uc-davis-football/>

21: Collins, Jim. *Good to Great: Why Some Companies Make the Leap...and Others Don't*. Harper Business, 2001. Print.

22: Byrne, Rhonda. *The Secret*. Atria Books/Beyond Words, 2006. Print.

23: Happyliving.com: "The Nature of Luck- a Happy Living Update". Web. <http://www.happyliving.com/2015/08/12/the-nature-of-luck-a-happy-living-update/>

24: Happyliving.com: "My Philosophy for Lifelong Work". Web. <http://www.happyliving.com/2014/11/12/lifelong-work-financial-fitness/>

25: Jimcollins.com: "The Hedgehog Concept". Web. <http://www.jimcollins.com/media_topics/hedgehog-concept.html>

26: Wikipedia.com: "Microform". Web. <https://en.wikipedia.org/wiki/Microform>

27: Ritholtz.com: "The Shift from Manufacturing to Service Economy". Web.

<http://www.ritholtz.com/blog/2012/01/the-shift-from-manufacturing-to-service-economy/>
28: Wikipedia.com: "White Paper". Web.
<https://en.wikipedia.org/wiki/White_paper>
29: Gdmllc.com: "The New Normal". Web.
<https://www.gdmllc.com/webinars/30/The_New_No rmal.pdf>
30: Wikipedia.com: "Type A and Type B personality theory". Web.
<https://en.wikipedia.org/wiki/Type_A_and_Type_B_ personality_theory>
31: "Rascal Flatts - Bless the Broken Road - Official Video." YouTube. June 3 2008. Web.
<https://www.youtube.com/watch?v=7a47fEuB9vo>
32: Wattpad.com: "How to Find Your Soulmate".
Web.<https://www.wattpad.com/88302-how-to-find-your-soulmate>
33: Pressfield, Steven. *The Warrior Ethos*. Black Irish Entertainment, LLC 2011. Print.
34: Wikipedia.com: "Alexander the Great". Web.
<https://en.wikipedia.org/wiki/Alexander_the_Great>
35: Hawkins, David R. MD, PHD. Power vs Force. Hay House Inc, 2014. Print.
36: Pressfield, Steven. *The Warrior Ethos*. Black Irish Entertainment, LLC 2011. Print.
37: Dyer, Wayne, DR. *Change Your Thoughts - Change Your Life: Living the Wisdom of the Tao*. Hay House, 2009. Print.
38. Singer, Michael A. *The Untethered Soul: The Journey Beyond Yourself*. New Harbor Publications/ Noetic Books, 2007. Print.

39. Wikipedia.com: "Ikigai". Web.
<https://en.wikipedia.org/wiki/Ikigai>
40. The Secret. (2006). [DVD].
41: Happyliving.com: "Magnificence & My Philosophy on Significance". Web.
<http://www.happyliving.com/2015/03/25/spirituality/>
42: Singer, Michael A. *The Untethered Soul: The Journey Beyond Yourself*. New Harbor Publications/ Noetic Books, 2007. Print.
43: Wikipedia.com: "Flow (psychology)". Web.
<http://en.wikipedia.org/wiki/Flow_(psychology)>
44: "UC Davis Football Coach Talk." YouTube. June 9 2014. Web.
<https://www.youtube.com/watch?v=2APpuJh9s6I&feature=youtu.be>
45: Happyliving.com: "Something Significant: One Simple Thing – The Legacy of U.C. Davis Football"
<http://www.happyliving.com/2015/02/04/something-significant-uc-davis-football/>
46: Jackson, Phil. *Sacred Hoops: Spiritual Lessons of a Hardwood Warrior*. Hachette Books; Reissue Edition, 2006. Print.
47: Wikipedia.com: "Jim Sochor". Web.
<https://en.wikipedia.org/wiki/Jim_Sochor>
48: Gersper, Matt and Sues, Kaileen. *The Belief Road Map.* Happy Living Books Independent Publishing, 2016. Print.
49: Singer, Michael A. *The Untethered Soul: The Journey Beyond Yourself*. New Harbor Publications/ Noetic Books, 2007. Print.

50: Ming-Dao, Deng. *The Lunar Tao: Meditations in Harmony with the Seasons*. HarperOne 2013. Print.

51: Buford, Bob P. *Halftime: Moving from Success to Significance*. Zondervan, 2008. Print.

52: Grandcanyonlodges.com: "Nestled at the Bottom of Grand Canyon". Web. < http://www.grandcanyonlodges.com/lodging/phantom-ranch/>

53: *The MacArthur Study Bible*, New King James Version. Print.

54: Happyliving.com: "My Philosophy for Lifelong Exercise". Web. <http://www.happyliving.com/2014/09/17/philosophy-lifelong-exercise/>

55: Happyliving.com: "Premium Gasoline and Junk Food – My Nutritional Philosophy". Web. <http://www.happyliving.com/2014/10/08/premium-gasoline-junk-food-nutritional-philosophy/>

56: Happyliving.com: "Sleep Better, Lose Weight, and Live Longer with Melatonin". Web. <http://www.happyliving.com/2014/07/30/melatonin/>

57: Happyliving.com: "Measuring for Improvement". Web. <http://www.happyliving.com/2014/08/06/measuring-improvement/>

58: Happyliving.com: "More Efficient and Effective Reading with Kindle". Web. <http://www.happyliving.com/2015/08/26/more-efficient-and-effective-reading-with-kindle/>

59: Happyliving.com: "The Simply Amazing Happy Living Pill". Web. <http://www.happyliving.com/2014/10/29/simply-amazing-happy-living-pill/>

60: Happyliving.com: "Seven Steps for Goal Setting". Web. <http://www.happyliving.com/2014/06/18/seven-steps-goal-setting/>

61: Happyliving.com: "Ideas for Turning Inward". Web. <http://www.happyliving.com/2014/09/05/ideas-turning-inward/>

62: Happyliving.com: "My Philosophy for Lifelong Work". Web. <http://www.happyliving.com/2014/11/12/lifelong-work-financial-fitness/>

63: Happyliving.com: "Unexpected Kindness". Web. <http://www.happyliving.com/2014/09/10/unexpected-kindness/>

64: Happyliving.com: "Bits of Inspiration- Self Care". Web. <http://www.happyliving.com/2014/08/15/self-care/>

65: Happyliving.com: "My Philosophy on Adventure and Unknown Outcomes". Web. <http://www.happyliving.com/2015/10/14/adventure-and-unknown-outcomes/>

66: Happyliving.com: "My Philosophy on Adventure and Continuous Exploration". Web. <http://www.happyliving.com/2015/10/21/my-philosophy-on-adventure-and-continuous-exploration/>

67: Happyliving.com: "Ideas for Happier Living". Web. <http://www.happyliving.com/2014/05/09/ideas-happier-travel/>
68: Happyliving.com: "Special Announcement: Epic Adventure in Cozumel, Mexico". Web. <http://www.happyliving.com/2014/10/31/epic-adventure-cozumel/>
69: Happyliving.com: "My Philosophy on Significance and Leaving Your Mark". Web. <http://www.happyliving.com/2015/08/19/my-philosophy-on-significance/>
70: Gersper, Matt and Sues, Kaileen. *The Belief Road Map*. Happy Living Books Independent Publishing, 2016. Print.
71: Hamilton, Laird. *Force of Nature: Mind, Body, Soul (and of Course Surfing)*. Rodale, 2010. Ebook.
72: Happyliving.com: "How to Maximize the Benefits of Any Conference-Paleo F(x) 2015". Web. <http://www.happyliving.com/2015/05/06/maximize-the-benefits-of-any-conference/>
73: Happyliving.com : "The Seven Foundations of Health". Web. <http://www.happyliving.com/2014/11/07/seven-foundations-of-health/>
74: Wikipedia.com: "Mind map". Web. <https://en.wikipedia.org/wiki/Mind_map>
75: Happyliving.com: "My Philosophy for Lifelong Work". Web. <http://www.happyliving.com/2014/11/12/lifelong-work-financial-fitness/>

76: Goodreads.com: "William Hutchison Murray > Quotes> Quotable Quote". Web. <http://www.goodreads.com/quotes/128689-until-one-is-committed-there-is-hesitancy-the-chance-to>
77: Lin, Derek. *The Tao of Joy Every Day: 365 Days of Tao Living.* TarcherPerigee, 2011. Ebook.
78: Tzu, Lao. *Tao Te Ching: The New Translation from Tao Te Ching: The Definitive Edition* (Tarcher Cornerstone Editions). TarcherPerigee, 2003. Print.
79: Gersper, Matt and Sues, Kaileen. *The Belief Road Map.* Happy Living Books Independent Publishing, 2016. Print.
80. Gladwell, Malcom. *Outliers: The Story of Success.* Back Bay Books, 2011. Print.
81: Coelho, Paulo. *The Alchemist.* HarperOne, 2015. Ebook.
82: Wikipedia.com: "Paul Hawken". Web. <https://en.wikipedia.org/wiki/Paul_Hawken>
83: Wikipedia.com: "Billy Joel". Web. < https://en.wikipedia.org/wiki/Billy_Joel>
84: Happyliving.com: "The Nature of Luck- a Happy Living Update". Web. <http://www.happyliving.com/2015/08/12/the-nature-of-luck-a-happy-living-update/>

About the Author

Matt Gersper
Author | Speaker |
Entrepreneur

On a mission to improve the health and wellbeing of the world, one person at a time.

Founder, HappyLiving.com & Happy Living Books Independent Publishing

Hi, I'm Matt Gersper!

I live on Lake Norman in Mooresville, North Carolina with my beautiful wife and our two daughters, and I also have two wonderful grown up children and have recently become a very proud Grandpa.

I graduated from the University of California - Davis where I studied Economics, ran track, and played football. I dedicated my first two years after college to becoming a professional athlete, only to come up short with the unique distinction of being cut from three different teams, in three different leagues: Canadian, USFL, and NFL.

Over the next 30 years, I focused on training myself to become a successful businessman. I was given many opportunities to learn and gain expertise in the various functions required to start, grow, and lead successful businesses.

On January 16, 2014, I decided to sell my previous company and dedicate my time and resources to researching and sharing best practices for happy living, shifting my focus from helping businesses to helping people.

I write to inspire others to believe that a better self is always possible – today, every day, for the rest of their lives.

Join Us at Happy Living

Be advised of upcoming books and updates from Happy Living! We are on a mission to improve the health and wellbeing of the world, one person at a time. Our blog is packed full of ideas for living with health, abundance, and compassion. Go to www.happyliving.com to sign up for your free membership.

Thank You!

Thank you for reading Turning Inspiration into Action!

If you enjoyed this book, please leave a kind REVIEW on Amazon.com!

Wishing you every success in life that you can imagine...

Matt Gersper
matt@happyliving.com